RECLAIMING *your* COMMUNITY

YOU DON'T HAVE TO MOVE OUT OF YOUR NEIGHBORHOOD TO LIVE IN A BETTER ONE

MAJORA CARTER

BK

Berrett–Koehler Publishers, Inc.

Berrett-Koehler Publishers, Inc.
1333 Broadway, Suite 1000
Oakland, CA 94612-1921
Tel: (510) 817-2277
Fax: (510) 817-2278
www.bkconnection.com

ORDERING INFORMATION
Quantity sales. Special discounts are available on quantity purchases by corporations, associations, and others. For details, contact the Special Sales Department at the Berrett-Koehler address above.
Individual sales. Berrett-Koehler publications are available through most bookstores. They can also be ordered directly from Berrett-Koehler: Tel: (800) 929-2929; Fax: (802) 864-7626; www.bkconnection.com.
Orders for college textbook / course adoption use. Please contact Berrett-Koehler: Tel: (800) 929-2929; Fax: (802) 864-7626.

Distributed to the U.S. trade and internationally by Penguin Random House Publisher Services.

Berrett-Koehler and the BK logo are registered trademarks of Berrett-Koehler Publishers, Inc.

Printed in Canada

Berrett-Koehler books are printed on long-lasting acid-free paper. When it is available, we choose paper that has been manufactured by environmentally responsible processes. These may include using trees grown in sustainable forests, incorporating recycled paper, minimizing chlorine in bleaching, or recycling the energy produced at the paper mill.

Library of Congress Cataloging-in-Publication Data

Names: Carter, Majora, author.
Title: Reclaiming your community : you don't have to move out of your
  neighborhood to live in a better one / Majora Carter.
Description: 1 Edition. | Oakland, CA : Berrett-Koehler, 2022. | Includes
  bibliographical references and index.
Identifiers: LCCN 2021034194 (print) | LCCN 2021034195 (ebook) | ISBN
  9781523000296 (hardcover) | ISBN 9781523000302 (adobe pdf) | ISBN
  9781523000319 (epub)
Subjects: LCSH: Community development--United States. | Ability--United
  States.
Classification: LCC HN90.C6 C366 2022 (print) | LCC HN90.C6 (ebook) | DDC
  307.1/40973—dc23
LC record available at https://lccn.loc.gov/2021034194
LC ebook record available at https://lccn.loc.gov/2021034195

First Edition
27 26 25 24 23 22 21   10 9 8 7 6 5 4 3 2 1

Book producer: PeopleSpeak
Text designer: Reider Books
Cover designer: Mike Nicholls
Cover art designer: Rush Humphrey
Author photo: Glass_from_the_past_\Roy Kimbrough

For my ancestors.
I will get caught trying because you did it first.

CONTENTS

PREFACE

Reclaiming our communities may sound like some utopian vision.

Others may hear a threatening war cry.

To me, it should be the standard operating procedure to promote peace and happiness in every community.

I consider "pray" and "hope" action verbs. "Reclaiming our communities" is my prayer and hope that all people in neighborhoods like the one I grew up in see the Divine in ourselves and the places we come from. That's not always an easy thing to do.

White supremacy, the media, public and private policies, and even local traditions and attitudes often lead us to believe that neither we nor our communities are worthy of consideration or respect. Despite all that, this book is an attempt to share my story of why I believe that the reclamation of those types of American communities, the very ones that have been written off as intractable problems that can never be solved, will advance human potential, save money, and soothe our own souls as well.

A major character in this book is my hometown, the South Bronx itself, and it bears the scars and spirits of ancestors and offenses gone but not forgotten.

I would like to pay my respects and acknowledge that the land where I grew up and still live, now called Hunts Point, in the South

Bronx in New York City was occupied by the Siwanoy people until Europeans invaded.

I would also like to acknowledge the descendants of Africans who were enslaved to toil for the White families on the pastoral estates that once dotted this landscape hundreds of years ago. They were blotted out of history until a group of schoolchildren from my alma mater, PS 48, discovered their remains.[1]

In its most recent history, where my life comes in, the South Bronx is a so-called inner city neighborhood—a national symbol of urban blight. I've spent the best parts of my adult life trying to rebuild the infrastructure in communities that sets up the conditions for love, peace, and belonging to flourish for others as well as myself. That is the ultimate goal of using the gifts that God gave me to help heal this crazy world in which we live.

My hope is that others will be ignited by a new way to think about and do community development. All have something to gain—and contribute—by considering this approach, whether they are community leaders, business leaders, government leaders, activists, educators, spiritual leaders, life coaches, counselors, startup and social entrepreneurs, real estate developers, economic development professionals, or any others who are yearning to structure a more equitable type of personal or professional relationship in community development.

James, my beautiful husband, groovy dance-skater, business partner, fellow conspirator in all the plans we make—the solid as well as the harebrained—and the best friend a girl could have (especially since he can cook so well), often tells me that I must be a little bit tortured because relaxing does not seem to be in my repertoire of activities I can do well, or at the very least like to do. I don't disagree.

My prayer and hope is that no one feels that they have to move out of their neighborhood to live in a better one. I do believe that encouraging that sentiment as a policy is a path forward for our society.

I work joyfully toward that goal daily in one way or another. And yes, I do pray and hope that others will use their own position, apply their own swagger, and follow suit.

And then, my inability to relax will not have been in vain. James and I can take a breather, and maybe he'll teach me to roller skate as well as he can.

GLOSSARY OF TERMS I USE

Here's a glossary of terms that I use throughout the book and what I mean when I use them:

fan club: These are one's haters. To paraphrase Kat Williams, an irreverent, wise, and hilarious soul: "If you only got fourteen haters, you better figure out how to get to sixteen before summer. Haters' job is to hate, so let them do their job. They keep people talking about you and make you famous." But seriously, if you are doing anything truly disruptive, it will irritate people in ways that even they can't articulate.

low-status: I first heard the term "low-status" used by danah boyd on a panel at a *Fast Company* event on April 29, 2015, and in her book *It's Complicated: The Social Lives of Networked Teens* on how video games have influenced culture. I was intrigued about the breadth of that concept and thought about how that term had more depth than the way communities like my own in the South Bronx were usually described: poor, underserved, disadvantaged, or low-income—all one dimensional and in my opinion, symptoms of an underlying condition of inequality.

I considered using the term "frontline" because people from those communities, like the canary in a coal mine, experience the first and the worst impacts of whatever is coming at them from climate change to income inequality. I decided against it because the imagery of people being attacked on the "front line" all the time is triggering to me, and it didn't necessarily indicate inequality either.

"Low-status," to me, simply illustrates the equality gap in a society without explicitly implicating racism, classism, or geography. These are places where inequality is assumed by those who live there and by everyone on the outside looking in. It is not a pretty sentiment, but it is a true one.

nonprofit industrial complex (NPIC): This is the combined collection of philanthropic and corporate funders, government agencies, and the nonprofit organizations that exist alongside, and often benefit from, the state of persistent inequality—even though many problems seem to get worse.

poverty-level economic maintenance (PLEM): This term refers to the type of developments that one finds in low-status communities, such as health clinics, "community centers," liquor stores, dollar stores, fast-food restaurants, check-cashing stores, pawn shops, and concentrations of very low-income subsidized affordable rental housing. Money is being made from these developments, but it does not circulate back into the local economy. It is an extractive commerce that drains capital out of communities and generally does not inspire loyalty among those that reside there.

INTRODUCTION
There Goes the Neighborhood

Imagine a thief in the night who came into your house, roused you from a deep, dreamless sleep, forced you out onto the street, and then slept in your bed. And there you are, standing on the sidewalk in the not-fit-to-be-seen-in-public T-shirt you went to sleep in, staring at your house, and wondering how *you* got to be considered a trespasser.

Did this thief just pop up out of nowhere, or were they a long time coming? Were there signs of their impending arrival? Did you get wind of talk that your neighborhood was "changing"?

Maybe you had heard about something like this happening in other neighborhoods. But here? Already?

The scenario above is a dramatic metaphor for how a community might experience what is commonly referred to as "gentrification"—or in other words, how poor people of color displaced by wealthier white people might feel.

The imagery came to mind as I reflected on the title of this book, *Reclaiming Your Community*, as well as a conversation I had wherein I heard the following quote: "You are not doing any favors by 'fixing' a person and then sending them back to a broken community."[1]

Statistically, living in an area of concentrated poverty is worse for poor people than living in economically diverse communities.[2] Your chances of a better life diminish if you're geographically concentrated with other impoverished people.[3]

So what is it that we want to "reclaim" and from whom?

Are we trying to reclaim communities from future development that will not be accessible? Does that mean preserving the less-than-satisfactory status quo in front of us now?

Can we reclaim a community from poverty and end long-term economic stagnation along with the hopelessness that accompanies it?

Is it possible to reclaim our communities from that constant yearning for greener pastures because we grew up wanting to leave the places we're from?

If you "reclaim" your community and some amount of genuine prosperity unfolds, where will all the poor people go? Is that your problem too, on top of everything else you want to see in your future?

I believe that many of us carry the scars of our collective history. I often wonder if the imagination of aspiration has been wrung out of us by the savage vanquish of Black Wall Streets in Tulsa, Oklahoma, and Wilmington and Durham, North Carolina, or the violence against Black and Brown lives and systemic denials of finance and education? Has the European and later US conquest of Native lands or the stigmatization of non-White Latino and Asian immigrants made us unable to see the value of what has been in front of us all along?

Many brilliant and meticulously researched articles and books have been written on how structural inequality and systemic racism grew hand in hand with capitalism and the culture that treats poor communities, especially communities of color, as less-than-second-class citizens—hindering or ripping from them their right to pursue the American Dream, whether it has a symbolic white picket fence or is an LLC.

This isn't one of those books.

However, I do hope mine will provide a more contemporary lens on the data that takes into account the ever increasing spending (and perennially unimpressive results) for the advancement of poor people in terms of social indicators related to poverty. In other words, we keep spending more with continuously less-than-positive results.

You may agree or disagree with all sorts of things I say, but it's hard to argue that we should keep doing more of the same. It might be interesting to at least explore the possibility of a different approach, and that's what I am offering.

What you'll get here are my own experiences of community development in my hometown of Hunts Point in the South Bronx and seeing the joy, promise, and pragmatic utility of investing there emotionally, spiritually, *and* financially. I want to share some of my own conclusions about how America can come closer to its incredible promise by helping those born and raised there see the value of our hometowns and leveraging that value to bring others along.

I am a lifelong witness to the constant churn of impoverished families and individuals that stream through communities like mine. I was born into one of them. Myriad programs attempt to cater to their needs, but the affects of the *concentration* of poverty on the social, health, educational, and environmental outcomes of communities go seemingly unaddressed by the very systems sworn to impact it.

Given the amount of media, government, and philanthropic attention paid to the social problems of communities like mine, it's no wonder that at least some of their constituents defy the odds. Of course they do! And who doesn't love the Cinderella story of the _____ kid from the hood (fill in the blank with "brainy," "artistic," "athletic," etc.) born and raised in a hardscrabble community who grows up to be *somebody*!

These individual success stories emerge from those communities frequently, but most of these hometown heroes leave. We are taught to measure success by how far we get away from our own communities.

I understand that these are not most of the people in a community, but they are not nobody either—and even a small number of these success stories can play a pivotal role in the well-being of their hometown.

When our communities do not retain this group, their day-to-day examples of success are lost as well as their consumer spending and their longer term reinvestment resources and acumen. We lose the building blocks of those Black Wall Streets to other places that don't need them like we do and, in some cases, don't even want them.

Can we take steps to encourage those neighbors to feel invested in the future of their own hometown?

I draw on the type of projects that very few expect to see in a low-income community of color, built long before the typically understood development cycle, which assumes that those types of projects don't happen until gentrification is well underway. I've created national-award-winning parks, tech social enterprises, and cafes to divert people from the well-trodden path leading out of our community, and I have been with others around the world doing the same.

How about this?

Can we reclaim our communities from the notion that they will be either ghettos or displacement stories?

Can we reclaim our communities from hopelessness and exodus and guide them to a future of retained wealth and reinvestment?

What if we were to reclaim our communities from the pernicious and generational peril of brain drain? What might we have then?

Again, I am compelled to ask, What would we be "reclaiming" and from whom?

Let's take a look.

CHAPTER 1

MEASURING SUCCESS BY HOW FAR YOU GET AWAY FROM YOUR COMMUNITY

The woman's folded arms provided a shelf for her boobs as she leaned on her windowsill. Her window was on the ground floor of the apartment building on my corner. I don't remember what she looked like or even her name, but she was always enrobed in a flowered housecoat, perched at her window when I came home from school.

She didn't seem to know the given names of any of us kids, but she knew who our parents were and which buildings we lived in. She knew whether we were the troublemakers or the quiet ones or something in between. After making eye contact—because she wanted to make sure you knew exactly whom she was talking to even if she didn't address you by name—she would yell out all sorts of things at us as we passed by.

Boy, I saw your momma today. Miss Garcia said you better get straight on home and stop messing with them no-good boys. They ain't gone do nuttin but bring you and your momma and papi trouble. G'awn now.

5

Miss Carter ain't got nuttin to worry 'bout witchu. She whoop your butt good if you do like the rest a these fast girls, but you got a good head on your shoulders—she say you got a honor mention in that *Highlight* magazine? Keep it up! Thank ya, Jesus!

She was one of the cast of characters that made up my neighborhood. I was fascinated that someone learned so much about other people by keeping her head stuck out a window while wearing a housecoat. I literally never saw what her lower body looked like.

Her building had a little courtyard in the center of it that separated the building into two sections. The side she didn't live in was mostly abandoned because it had been torched earlier that summer. People were still living in some of the apartments that escaped the flames, smoke, and water, although they had to walk down stairs past floors where apartments had been burned out. Squatters, sometimes drug dealers, had taken over some of them.

It took what seemed like hours for the fire department to get there when the building was actually burning. Nobody blamed them. Firehouses were being closed all around New York City and in Black and Latino neighborhoods especially, so neighbors pitched in as they could.

I saw Peto, a young man whose family lived two doors down from mine, carefully helping a very old lady down the fire escape. Others helped too, but I remember Peto the most. He was so gentle with that lady, who could clearly not move very fast, and he got her down safely. He was and still is a hero to me.

Some believed the building was torched by the landlord to get insurance money. Others said it was started accidentally by the kids in a family full of mean kids that lived in the building.

Those kids didn't seem to have any adult supervision; they were always beating up on someone, and they knew how to fight dirty. I saw one of them bite the cheek of another kid. Even though the skin wasn't broken, there was a nasty-looking bruise there for weeks.

I took no chances. Even though I was tall for my age, I had never even thrown a punch and wasn't keen on trying, especially with that family. I would cross to the other side of the street whenever I saw any of them coming.

Either way, the mean-kid family was burned out of their apartment and I never saw any of them again.

Later that summer, the side of the building with Miss Housecoat was torched as well. And overnight, she was gone too.

It was August 23, 1974. One of the cops was a little paunchy with sandy blond, greasy-looking hair. His skin was slightly pockmarked. He had a kind but worried expression on his face—probably because my mother was crying softly, leaning into my father's shoulder. Another cop was there, but I don't remember him at all.

I was seven. I crouched down and peeked around the door of the living room, hoping that they wouldn't see me. I heard snippets of the conversation.

I knew that my beautiful big brother, Lenny, was dead—shot in the head above the left eye.

The cops were trying to understand how he ended up where he was, what got him killed. It was "suspicious." One of them asked my parents if they could search his room.

I scurried back to my bedroom before they started to move and took a post just inside the door. I couldn't hear anything they were saying in the other room, but I convinced myself that Lenny was in the top bunk and that the kind but worried cop just so happened to be a surgeon and was extracting the bullet from above his left eye and Lenny would therefore, miraculously, come back to life.

That fantasy lasted about two minutes as my other family members started to wake up.

Lenny had what is now commonly known as PTSD (post-traumatic stress disorder). Once, I overheard my mother telling her friend Ms. Mattie that when she went to wake him up for his shift with the US Postal Service, he jumped out of bed and lunged at her as if she were a Vietcong soldier. Thank God he didn't sleep with a gun, she'd said.

Many years later, I discovered that my brother, like some young men in the South Bronx and other poor communities of color around the country, got caught up in the illegal drug trade in the late 1960s–1970s.

Lenny served two combat tours in Vietnam. I wish I could find the letters that he wrote to me in his perfect penmanship. He would enclose little gifts for me in the envelope, like a handwoven ribbon made in Vietnam that I wore as a headband around my tiny little afro.

I was so happy when he wrote that he was coming home and wouldn't have to go back to that vicious war that I saw on the news. Unlike the rest of my siblings, he never made fun of me for being an awkward little bookworm, tall for my age with an afro that never grew beyond an inch in the era of big afros.

Sometimes, Lenny rode me on the handlebars of his bike, let me hang out with him even when his friends came over, and led me to believe that I was a graceful dancer worthy of the most skillful *Soul Train* line—I definitely was not, but I liked hearing him say it.

Lenny was my brother.
A very good brother, indeed.
But he's dead now,
Killed with the slightest of ease.
I was crying at his funeral wishing he were back,
But he's in the hands of the Lord now
And he cannot come back.

I wrote that poem for him shortly after his murder.

I knew what to do. I had a good head on my shoulders after all; the lady in the housecoat confirmed what I already knew to be true.

At the age of seven years and ten months, I was determined to grow up and get out of there. I started planning my escape from The Bronx.

CHAPTER 2

GEEKY LITTLE KID
IN THE GHETTO

W hen school started again, after the summer of my brother's unsolved murder, I sat next to J. in Mr. Dombrow's third grade class at PS 48 just as the rest of the class was settling in.

J. was a lithesome, pretty, brown-skinned girl, always dressed in fashionable clothes. She was partial to bell bottoms with embroidery on them. She was the cool third grade Black girl version of Marcia Brady. Her thick, long hair was neatly done in two double-stranded ponytails that grazed her shoulders, and elastics with plastic marbles secured her hair at the root and the ends.

I felt like a hulking beast next to her. I wore sensible dark blue "Marty" shoes from Buster Brown that my mom insisted on getting because they were indestructible. I know they were because I tried to destroy them—many times. I dragged the toes on pavement and scraped the sides along curbs. "Nothing a little navy blue shoe polish won't fix!" my mom would say, delighted by the outcome of her thriftiness. When I outgrew a pair, they would be replaced by yet another.

I wore the one new outfit that my mom bought me for the first day of the school year. I am pretty sure it was bought at either the Robert Hall or the Great Eastern department store. It wasn't anything

like the fashion show that J. put on at the beginning of every school
semester. It seemed to me that she never wore the same outfit twice
in the first month of school. I knew that tomorrow, I'd be back in
hand-me-downs from my sisters or brothers, anywhere from three to
sixteen years older than me. My clothes were outdated before I even
put them on.

But J. had always been nice and chatty to me, despite my bad fashion sense. She told me she wouldn't be seeing me anymore soon. Her
family was moving to New Rochelle.

She shared that her parents said the neighborhood was getting
bad and they didn't want her in it anymore. Their new home wasn't
ready by the time school started, but she assured me it was really nice
and her new school was too.

"How was *your* summer?" she asked.

"My brother got killed."

"*Welcome to third grade!*" Mr. Dombrow announced. I was glad he
started the class.

J. and I never spoke of my brother's murder again and within the
month, she was gone—another one of the sirens that signaled all was
not right in my neighborhood.

There were many sirens. After a while, you barely heard them
anymore, despite their growing frequency.

Early in our courtship, my husband, James, and I told each other
about our childhoods.

He told me that he rode horses and motorcycles, that his first girl-
friend was also his closest neighbor and her family lived over a mile
away, and that there were more cows than people in his hometown in
rural Wisconsin.

I told him about my brother's murder, the fires, and investigating
with my friends the bloodstain that was left in an alley after a junkie
fell or was thrown from a roof.

Despite his small-town roots, he has traveled the world and
speaks several languages. More than one of his trips took him into
intense conflict zones in Nicaragua and Colombia as well as on ocean

crossings on small sailboats. So it meant something to me when his big brown eyes got even bigger and he said gently, "It sounds like you grew up in a war zone."

Hmmm. I never thought of my life that way, but I could see why someone else would.

When I had that exchange with J., I was almost eight years old—a bit too old to admit that I still loved *Mister Rogers' Neighborhood*, I thought. The serenity in the Neighborhood of Make-Believe was like a meditative state that I could retreat to when I needed to abide my introverted tendencies.

Funny enough, my life did have elements of Mister Rogers's neighborhood. Despite the trauma caused by losing people and places I loved, I never felt unsafe as a child in Hunts Point.

Safety—not the first thing that the South Bronx would bring to mind when anyone who knew about the South Bronx would think about it. But as a little kid, the blocks around my house were the beginning and end of my own happy universe.

My life was going to school and soaking up all the knowledge I could from my favorite teachers, running home, doing my homework, putting on my play clothes, and then playing street games like double Dutch, skelsies, and stickball with my friends in the middle of the street outside our houses, grudgingly moving out of the way when cars needed to pass. And there were the occasional packs of roving stray dogs that were a little scary at times.

I remember that when it started to get dark, the mothers on the block would call their kids inside for dinner. My mom had a particular whistle that I can remember to this day: two identical short tones and then a sharper, even shorter one.

I was the youngest of ten kids. My father was twenty-one years older than my mom.

When they married, he had three sons about her age and she had three kids under six years old. After my dad moved my mom and her kids to Hunts Point, they had four more together. We were the ghetto Brady Bunch.

By the time I was born, six of us kids still lived at home and we all sat down to dinner together, frequently joined by friends and neighbors from far and wide. Our home was a happy sanctuary to me and many others.

Daddy was a news junkie, often flipping between the three major networks available at that time in case there were different takes on the news. There really weren't.

Even though we now have many more opportunities to find out about current events, and they are increasingly polarized by both progressive and conservative media outlets, it never ceases to amaze me about how the same news stories get recycled over and over again. It was the same back then.

Figures 1 and 2 show the kind of images that appeared on the nightly news programs that I watched with my dad. This is how I learned that my neighborhood was nationally known as the poster child for urban blight.

FIGURE 1: Building in Hunts Point, South Bronx, 1989

FIGURE 2: Students of PS 48 in Hunts Point, South Bronx, 1989
Source: "Our Hope Shines Brightly: A Photo-Essay on Our Environment," class 4-5,
PS 48, The Bronx, NY, 1989, Gail David, teacher and advisor.

These photos were taken in Hunts Point by students in Ms. Gail David's fourth grade class at PS 48 in 1989. The neighborhood looked about the same a dozen years prior when I was their age.

Many years later, I learned from Ms. David that her students were part of the United Nations Environment Programme's Youth Forum on the Environment in 1989 and presented these photos for their own exhibition at the UN Assembly. The text accompanying the exhibition read that the students' project was "a testimony to the desire for a better future that looms large and possible, as seen through our eyes."

Ms. David and her colleagues contacted every media outlet in New York City, but no one picked up the story. According to this dedicated educator who was so passionate about her students' ability to shine, the reporters and editors cited that the story was "not sensational enough."

In the era when The Bronx was burning and crack was an epidemic, kids who could *still* see hope and possibility must have seemed like they were on a fool's errand or simply unbelievable.

The World Is Watching Us Burn

Back in 1977, I watched one of the World Series games while visiting my grandmother in Philadelphia. The game played on the ancient black-and-white TV perched in the corner of Grandma's living room. I sat on the floor as my family watched the game.

At one point, the camera hovering above Yankee Stadium panned out, and sportscaster Howard Cosell provided gravelly commentary. They bore witness to three separate buildings in The Bronx on fire at once.

I was eleven years old. None of the fires shown that night were in my neighborhood, but in my short life, I had seen enough buildings burn, walked through their shells on a dare, and crossed through the rubble of what was once the homes of people living their lives because it was a shortcut to wherever I was going.

I sat on Grandma's floor, legs splayed out in front of me, and it felt like I had vomited inside my own body. Seeing and hearing this during a big event like a World Series game made me feel so humiliated, embarrassed, and sickened by the fact that the entire *world* was watching my hometown burn.

I knew what everyone must have thought of us, what they thought of anyone from The Bronx, the South Bronx especially, since that was where all the Blacks and Latinos (almost all Puerto Ricans back then) lived. In my mind, they were screaming things like this about us:

Nothing there but pimps, dope dealers, gangs, drug addicts, and prostitutes! Burning down their own buildings! Living in piles of garbage! Those slums should be cleared! The schools are crap! They don't care about their kids! They don't even care enough about themselves to care about anything!

"Three more years," I thought. "In three years, I will take the New York City specialized high school entrance exam. I will get into the Bronx High School of Science, and that will be my ticket out of that place."

From the late 1960s to the 1980s, the South Bronx suffered from a disproportionate number of fires, which were blamed on accidents, faulty wiring, fire department budget cutbacks, and landlords committing arson because the economics of the times made it more profitable to collect insurance money than reinvest in those buildings.[1] All the reasons for the burning have been the subject of much debate regarding which had the most impact on the breakdown of the social, environmental, or economic security of the South Bronx over the ensuing decades.

I reckon it was a toxic combination of all of the above, the end result being a community neglected, misunderstood, and vilified by policies, practices, actions, and attitudes of those from outside and inside the community.

Well-documented discriminatory and destructive financial practices by the banking industry still plague our community.

Our country's governments at all levels have a long and shameful history of creating policies and overtly carrying out projects that have brutalized communities of color. It's not a mystery because they put it all in writing:

- Pushing highway construction through communities of color
- Siting noxious infrastructure developments along race and class lines
- Eroding quality education and healthcare access
- Poorly maintaining public parks
- Resisting positive economic development

While her husband's administration looked the other way when smugglers were bringing drugs into the country as a side effect of the Iran-Contra deal and subsequent scandal, First Lady Nancy Reagan demurred, "Just Say No." No wonder why many in poor communities believe that the illegal drug trade was guided into poor Black and Latino communities by our government as a tool to destabilize us.

All of the above and other issues have played a role in truncating the ability of residents of the South Bronx and other "inner-city" American communities like it to prosper.

Of course, I wanted to get the hell out of there. As I was one of the best students, it was expected. There was a general sense that nothing good stayed in neighborhoods like the one we were born and raised in.

Kids like me were the epitome of brain drain.

Planning Escape

Being from the South Bronx left you with a stain that marked you as less-than. The South Bronx meant pimp, pusher, or prostitute to most of America at the time, and I internalized that. Like most smart kids, I used education as my escape.

Mr. Ruckstahl, Ms. Galvin, Mr. Dorogusker, Mr. Vasquez, and others, were eighth grade teachers who tutored a select group of their high-achieving students, including me, to help us pass the entrance exam for New York City's specialized high schools.

I did test into the Bronx High School of Science and went on to Wesleyan University, my first choice, and graduate school at New York University. But my shame accompanied me throughout my school trajectory. It would show up with a smirk and a nod, reminding me that my background was always present and nobody liked it.

On a college visit to Wesleyan, for example, I was cornered by two older male students. They were both Black. One was from The Bronx. In my mind, and I am sure in his too, he was from a neighborhood far nicer than mine.

"So, where are you from?"

"New York."

"Where in New York?"

"New York City."

"Where in New York City?"

"The Bronx."

"Oh yeah? Where?"

"The southeast part."

"What's the name of your neighborhood?"

"It's . . . Hunts Point."

"Oh. That's where all the prostitutes come from."

I never saw them again. Or maybe I actively blocked them from my consciousness.

I became skilled at finding ways to change the subject when asked where I was from.

To be fair, far more students could not have cared less about where I was from. But I was trying to navigate my way out of a place that had been written off.

I felt as if erasing ties to my community was my only way to lead a life where I wasn't defined by the worst elements from my hometown.

CHAPTER 3

CONDITIONS FOR BRAIN DRAIN
How to Disinvite Your Hometown Heroes

Bloggers Alex and Lara Lill explain how monocultures go against nature's plan of biodiversity:

> In the natural world, we see all kinds of species *co-existing* and *depending* on one another for growth and survival. This is biodiversity. Every species has a vital role to play within the ecosystems on Earth. Diversity among species ensures natural sustainability for all life forms and a much higher defense against disasters. . . .
>
> A monoculture is an immense amount of land, planted with one species of crop. . . .
>
> Monocultures create a quicker buildup of diseases and pests, which is just one reason why they have been criticized for their negative effects on the environment. . . .
>
> Nature spelled it out for us: Biodiversity is the key to survival.[1]

Monocultures are vulnerable. Think of the disease that caused the Irish potato famine. I believe that the built environment of low-status communities creates *economic* monocultures. That practice leads to concentrated poverty and every social issue associated with it.

By "low-status" I mean the places where it is widely agreed that the schools are worse, the air is more polluted, the parks are few and less well maintained, the health statistics are not good, and the elected officials and nonprofit industrial complex readily acknowledge that these disparities exist but seem unable to address them with any effectiveness. These places are not unique to any race. They can be urban, rural, or suburban areas, inner cities, Native American reservations, or formerly booming Rust Belt or mining towns, among others.

Monocultures represent vulnerability, while diversity represents resiliency.

The term "brain drain" is generally assumed to mean the emigration of highly trained or intelligent people from a particular country, but brain drain happens in American low-status communities too. Public policies, internal and external attitudes and biases, and the built environment of low-status communities actively encourage a crucial portion of the population to measure their personal success by how far they get away from the community that they were born and raised in.

To continue the metaphor of monocultures, when a thriving diverse ecosystem experiences a loss of the right habitat or perhaps a small population of a pivotal species, it becomes more vulnerable. In low-status communities, that species loss is the equivalent of brain drain driven by habitat destruction. Low-status communities have never had a shortage of successful people *emerging* from those communities; we have had a shortage of them *staying* there.

The monoculture of inequality persists in low-status communities because of a talent-retention deficit.

How We Repel Talent

I run an urban revitalization strategy consulting company, and although I work nationally, my dream was always to apply my talents to my own neighborhood, so we conducted a community assessment survey in my neighborhood to better understand what was motivating people. In other words, what were their hopes, dreams, and aspirations for the life they wanted to lead?

More than five hundred people responded, and the data indicated that folks didn't want to leave the area for the reasons that those outside the community might expect, such as the high crime rates.[2]

Indeed, our community is not without its problems, but for the most part, violent crime rates have been dropping since the 1980s. Mostly, people left (or hoped to leave) to satisfy their lifestyle needs.

For example, we surveyed high school students on track to graduate who believed they would be successful after graduating college. When we asked them what the neighborhood was in need of, they tended to repeat the same litany: community centers, health clinics, programs for kids, affordable housing for the poorest people in the community, homeless shelters.

But when we asked them if they planned to use their future success to either come back or seek out another neighborhood with more of those things, their incredulity at such a question was palpable—they didn't want to live in places that have only community centers as their primary form of entertainment or have housing only for the most beleaguered in our society. These things were regarded as markers of poverty, and they wanted none of that. They fully intended to measure their success by how far they got away from the neighborhood.

Creating rental housing financed primarily by government subsidies for extremely low-income residents in low-status communities is not a bad deal for developers. And I have heard many elected officials and policymakers argue that pursuing a predominantly low-income rental housing–community center combo is in direct response to community needs. However, I have been hard-pressed to find anyone yearning to move on up and out of a low-status community who identified "community center" as high on the list of desirable amenities.

This concentration of government-subsidized affordable housing is a primary factor that entrenches a landless and transient class of people in low-status communities as it offers few reasons for those born and raised in the community who aspire to more for their own lives to want to stay and feel invested in their own hometown.

Think of the way that companies work to retain the talent they hire.

"I'm going to pour company time, money, and expertise into staff people, and then I am going to hand them over to my competitors," said no business owner ever.

Retaining positive and talented employees increases a business's chance for success, as well as morale and productivity, and well-cared-for employees will enjoy the benefits of seeing their hard work and contributions pay off for themselves and the company.[3] Interestingly enough, more money, which, of course, helps, is not always at the top of the list of why employees want to stay.

At our core, we want to feel appreciated and acknowledged, whether in a corporation or a community. If we don't get that recognition, we seek it elsewhere.

Low-status communities effectively operate as monocultures that subtly and overtly encourage the migration of many of its residents. So why don't we try to retain talent in low-status communities?

Going Beyond the Status Quo

Historically, we can find ample programs in low-status communities that have had the net effect of facilitating "brain drain." For example, "gifted and talented" tracks in public schools, college-readiness courses, and arts and sports programs are offered to the higher achieving young people in those communities.

The nonprofit, educational, and government sectors seem to uphold an unspoken duty to support the best and the brightest in those communities to grow up and get out, to help them measure success by how far they get away. They promote Cinderella stories of exceptionalism that are claimed as "success." This is not bad for the individuals in terms of the future life they are attempting to achieve. But how is expecting the talent born and raised in low-status communities to enrich someone else's neighborhood a good strategy for greater economic and cultural vibrancy? What has it produced so far other than a costly recipe for stagnation and decline?

What if we designed low-status communities to encourage the talent born and raised there to remain, similar to the way companies try to retain their talent? What would that look like? What would it require from all the parties involved? Would it be more costly or cheaper, and what might the results be?

If our goal was to keep the talent from leaving, we would have a different social and economic landscape in American low-status communities.

What if we made investments in the future wealth-generating capacity of residents, such as homeownership and business development, that address people's aspirations and not just the failure all around us? What if these communities had lifestyle infrastructure— so called *third spaces*—such as nice cafes, bars, restaurants, bookstores, and retail spaces, as well as more public options such as parks, greenways, and farmers markets?

In a community talent retention scenario, those community assets are to residents like company stock options are to employees of a company in that overall company or community success supports individual success.

Could lifestyle infrastructure encourage more people to stay and create opportunities for others in the neighborhood to realize their own potential because they see how other people like them have succeeded?

"Low income" is often associated with "neighborhood preservation" because poverty is mistakenly equated with culture. The nonprofit industrial complex and most government agencies seem to be disinclined to implement policies and projects that support the creation and retention of wealth and a better quality of life that is possible within low-status communities.

Instead, the well-intentioned efforts of activists, service providers, philanthropists, and the government often serve to repel talent. Their programmatic responses to community poverty statistics assume that low-status communities will always be poor, needy, and unsuccessful and thus in perpetual need of government and philanthropic largesse, to be turned on or off depending on external economic conditions that are always out of the control of those affected.

In my experience, "poverty" is also linked with "authenticity" in low-status communities. Those who don't fit a profile of desperation, whether an aspiring local entrepreneur or a homeowner, are not considered representative of the community and thus not planned for in any meaningful way. This fans the flames of talent exodus and a concentration of poverty.

For example, a local councilman in the South Bronx was vocal about vetoing any housing project that sought city funding if it wasn't 100 percent affordable.[4] Generally, such low-income rental subsidy programs are based on personal income and not geography. In other words, low-income rental housing serves to attract more poverty from other communities while not necessarily affecting the local population except to further concentrate poverty in areas that are already overburdened by these social and economic headwinds.

The net effect of activists, service providers, philanthropists, and the government continuing the long-standing status quo of interventions that support people *remaining* in poverty is that successful individuals born and raised in the communities are both subtly and actively encouraged to leave. And when these communities lose that talent,

- They lose day-to-day consumer spending dollars that can allow better businesses to grow.
- They lose everyday examples of success, making it harder to reach and teach the next generation and show them what is possible.
- They lose reinvestment capital in family homes that prior generations bought back when property values were low, during the era of White flight, urban renewal, and highway

construction. When they sell these hard-won assets, they eliminate any hope of passing that asset down to future generations.

Right now, aspiring people in those places have few opportunities from a housing and lifestyle perspective. They often exceed the income maximums for new low-income housing that is built in those neighborhoods. And I am not talking about people making six figures.

The income bands for many of these developments are so narrow that a family consisting of a bus driver and a teacher and their two kids makes too much money to live in many newer developments.[5] It doesn't matter if they're from the neighborhood and just want to be closer to their parents, who could help with childcare and whom they, in turn, could help as their parents age.

Building more housing dedicated to those members of the workforce can add stability to a community. On the other hand, building large quantities of exclusively low-income housing will continue the concentration of poverty.

You need more economic diversity, not less of it, to reverse the cycle that maintains high poverty levels. Many current housing practices do little to encourage or incentivize the more economically successful native residents to stay, grow, and share their example, which can enable a range of social connectivity that can inspire others to see that a better quality of life is possible within their own community.

To help better understand this situation, my company surveyed people in the community, via Google Forms on mobile devices (highly recommend—thanks, Google!) and focus groups (it helps to serve wine and dinner), and we learned what residents and commuters found attractive, what was missing for them, and what they did not like. Table 1 is a summary of some key points of that data.

We were not surprised to discover that folks in our community desired the same type of features that most people want: great places to live, good places to work, and nice cafes, bars, and restaurants. They expressed a disinclination toward and even aversion to readily

TABLE 1: Community survey results (excerpts)

Q: What are you looking for in the community you desire?	
A: Don't Want	**Want**
Health clinics/pharmacies	Coffee shop
"Community centers"	Family restaurants
Dog poop	Nice parks
Litter on street	Housing that matches my income
Homeless shelter	People like me (aspirational)

available things such as health clinics and pharmacies, people not picking up after their dogs, only cheap fast-food spots, liquor stores, and homeless shelters that attracted homeless and mentally ill people who were mostly from well outside their community.

People expressed a desire for things that represented their aspirations for themselves and the people they loved. Not surprisingly, plenty of respondents did not see much promise that the South Bronx would ever meet those aspirations and assumed en masse that they would have to leave the community to experience them. They were not confident that their community would affect their lives in a positive way. Fear of becoming a victim of violent crime was very rarely recorded in our surveys as a reason to leave.

Even though existing conditions people mentioned can diminish their chances for success, many of them still are successful. They have free will and can choose to spend their money accordingly. "Educating" people about the solidarity they "should" feel for their community and therefore deny themselves the quality of life they seek is not likely to affect individual decision-making in the marketplace. They need more day-to-day reminders that quality of life is achievable locally, such as the things listed above that they do want.

CHAPTER 4

WHEN EVERYTHING TELLS YOU THE SAME THING, YOU'LL PROBABLY BELIEVE IT

What motivated the domestic terrorists who invaded the Capitol on January 6, 2021; the mobs who carried out the massacre in the Black business district in Tulsa in 1921; the White supremacists who violently took over the government in Wilmington, North Carolina, in 1898; or the White men who tortured and killed fourteen-year-old Emmett Till for allegedly looking at a white woman the wrong way in 1955?

Treason. Destruction of property. Torture. Murder. Were these crimes committed to protect something the perpetrators felt was deserved or thought they would lose? Was fear a motivator?

The answer is likely all of my suppositions above as well as many others, but to me, more important than the actual answer is that the underlying foundation that supports these shameful and violent outbursts comes from a widespread and accepted belief in a racially unequal status quo.

With regard to people from low-status communities, that belief lives in folks from outside as well as those born and raised inside those communities. It has the overall effect of teaching people from low-status communities to believe that we and our surroundings are not worth much.

After I arrived at Wesleyan University as a freshman, I never saw the two upperclassmen (or should I say upperclassboys) who defined me only as prostitute-adjacent during my campus visit the previous year. Probably my subconscious blocked their appearance to avoid the humiliation I felt when it happened.

Less-than-ness. I just accepted it whenever thinking of my hometown and, by association, myself.

I felt that I was considered incomplete as a person because I was Black and from a neighborhood like the South Bronx. At the time, I had no real awareness about the role my gender played; that came later. All I really knew was that I was never going to be in league with White well-to-do people from places "better" than where I was from, no matter what.

I had received "the talk" from my parents and various family members and mentors about having to be twice as good and work twice as hard as my White peers just to get half as much. It was a talk familiar to any young Black person in America, immortalized by Kerry Washington, my fellow Bronxite, and Joe Morton in a scene between Olivia and her father, Rowan, in the television show *Scandal*. (Granted, most of us didn't have the talk delivered in an airplane hangar with our dad trying to force us on the private plane he secured so he could help us start a new life.)

Culture bearers like Black Twitter exploded in recognition and validation of the scene in *Scandal*, but mainstream media never seemed to quite understand the gravity of the talk and the lives of Black folks.[1] Again, my interest is not to analyze why folks do what they do but to illuminate what happens in the hearts and minds of those of us on the receiving end of those attitudes.

I don't think those Wesleyan boys willfully tried to make me feel ashamed of where I was from. There was nothing interesting or unique about them or what they did. They were simply adhering to the time-tested perception that "bad" neighborhoods and everything associated with them, including the people in them, deserve the stigma, ridicule, and disrespect.

Most of the neighbors I knew, like my family, were poor. And there were more drug addicts and prostitutes in my community than I saw in fancier parts of the city. However, I did notice that most of the cars that came to buy drugs or the services of prostitutes were driven by White men definitely not from around here.

Most of my neighbors were neither drug addicts nor prostitutes. Many people owned homes, they had families that they loved, and yes, those homes were nestled in between the burned out shells of buildings that dotted the landscape.

I accepted that my neighborhood had its problems, and I didn't have to work hard to imagine that something better was always happening outside of it. I was reminded of it all the time.

During one high school social studies class, one of my most beloved teachers, a White man, and one of my classmates, whose family emigrated from China, made light fun of the student's humble beginnings in America, which included first settling in the South Bronx. Something inside me burned hot as they laughed in relief and satisfaction about how happy they were that he'd made it "out"—and how far he'd come.

My fellow classmate was an unpleasant and awkward guy with a bad haircut and odd fashion sense. I had never been inclined to even look in his direction, but my teacher was a different story.

He had always seemed kind and was a good teacher to boot. I was hurt by his words, but I kept the pain neatly caged inside. It didn't occur to me to send it outward to make them understand how hurtful their comments were. I couldn't say anything because, after all, I believed the same about my neighborhood and wished my parents could have saved me from it the way that kid's parents had saved him.

Yearning for Relief

When I was a little girl still in the single digits, on most Sundays, my dad would go out in whatever Oldsmobile he had at the time and buy the Sunday *New York Times*. Newspaper distributors did not believe that the international paper of record would be of any real interest to our neighborhood, so my dad had to travel to a nicer neighborhood to find it.

When I discovered that there were listings of houses in upscale areas in the back pages of the *New York Times Magazine*, part of my Sunday morning ritual was placing the magazine with those pages open over the section of the paper my dad was reading and asking when we would go and see our future home.

Once I even went as far as calling one of the Realtors and requesting that they mail the floor plans for a listing to give my dad a better understanding of why that particular home would work well for us. I can't believe how patient my dad was with me or that the Realtor sent the plans at the request of an eight-year-old.

Occasionally, we would visit relatives out in Babylon, Long Island. Babylon was the type of place that Black folks who wanted to escape the ghetto yearned to move to. I know I did.

I thought my cousins lived in the lap of luxury. They had grass in their backyard and green parks nearby. It was in their backyard where I saw my first frog outside of a nature special on television. (Yeech.) There was a table in the kitchen and a whole separate dining room with an even bigger table!

It blew my mind whenever we visited.

Going home was always so hard. It would always be after dark and after extended goodbyes and hugs in my relatives' driveway.

I took the middle position in the front seat, scrunched between my mom and my dad, who was behind the wheel. I'm not even sure if the car had seat belts, but I know we didn't use them. It was the seventies, after all.

I would hide my sadness about leaving the palace I wanted to stay in by playing DJ with the eight-track player in the dashboard. I took requests from my four siblings in the backseat with the few tapes we had in the car, Barry White and Al Green among them.

I nestled my face in the soft, warm flesh of my mom's arm. She always smelled nice. Estée Lauder Private Collection.

We would wind through the suburban streets, eventually getting on the Whitestone Bridge to get back to The Bronx. My heart would sink a little bit more with each passing moment. Soon, the ghostly silhouettes of burned buildings would come into view—familiar, disappointing landscapes.

Daddy would turn the corner from Randall Avenue into our block on Manida Street. He would pass the ruins at the corner and continue up the street to 651.

He would pull into the driveway, everyone would spill out of the car, and one of my siblings would open the gate. I loved staying in the car while my dad maneuvered the car down the narrow driveway and into the parking space in our mostly concrete backyard. It felt like we were moving through a canyon.

The only nature left in our backyard consisted of the rosebushes and grapevines planted by the Saccos, the Italian family who lived in the house for two generations before my father bought it. The grape arbor had a canopy that covered about a third of the yard, at least ten feet by twenty-five feet. Seeing it always made me hopeful.

I spent a lot of time back there, creating art projects and exploring what lived in the raised beds. I would dig in the raised beds that the grapevines grew out of, examining interesting bugs. I steered clear of earthworms, respecting their place in the ecosystem but also being grossed out by them. Pill bugs were my favorite. They rolled into a ball when you touched them. My least favorite were common houseflies. I took great pleasure in capturing and killing them if they dared bother me during my backyard adventures. I would drown, burn, or squash them with gusto. They were nuisances.

My sister told me once that I woke up screaming in the middle of the night that flies were attacking me. I didn't remember it, but I did pull back on my fly-killing escapades. I no longer thought of creative ways to kill them, a simple swat became my go-to for the dignified end to a pest.

My mom supported all my artistic ventures in the backyard. I am pretty sure she didn't know about my fly murdering.

She would mix clay for me out of flour and water. I would press leaves and flowers into it, removing them after the clay was dry so I could paint the imprint they left. I was a crafty little one.

My time in the backyard—talking to bugs, reducing the fly population, creating nature art—was oasis time for me.

I knew from watching the news with my dad that my neighborhood was not a good place. Words like "violent," "gritty," "abandoned," "distressed," and "deprived" were not the words that anyone would use to describe a healthy community or the people in it, but they are a small sample of the words I heard used to describe us. How could that not have an impact on how you viewed yourself?

Even though I would often play street games with the kids on my block and never felt that my safety was an issue—except from falling off a homemade skateboard or tripping while jumping Double Dutch—I still had a foreboding sense that our neighborhood was just, well, bad.

When you grow up in a low-status community, an inferiority complex is baked into your psyche by everything around you. Both subtle and overt messages tell you that you will never truly measure up, and one way or another, you believe them.

CHAPTER 5

DARING TO NAME
OUR DREAMS

A name can be the embodiment of dreams deferred, longing to be made real.

That is what I believe now, but as a child I was simply fascinated by how Black folks, including my older relatives, had names that described a profession or title or a mythical being.

I knew of grown women and men named Queen, Princess, King, Prince.

Two of my mom's brothers were named Doctor and Hercules. My dad's name was Major.

I hated my name for most of my formative years. Mommy told me many times that I was supposed to have been named Julette, which combined the names of two people in my mom's life. The first was her sister, Julia, and the other was someone else I can never remember. I didn't really like Julette either. It sounded like a shaver, but it was *way* better than "Majora."

People had trouble pronouncing my name. I heard Marjorie, Myzora, Margarine, and others even more annoying. I had learned to sound words out when I was three, but for some reason, my name would stop most people dead in their speech tracks the second they saw it written or I introduced myself.

I was about four when I discovered that my father had a name that wasn't Daddy.

"Daddy! You named me after you!"

"No, I didn't. I named you after my sister, Aunt Marie, that's the *MA*. The *JO* is from my cousin, your Aunt Josephine, and the *R* is for Marie's sister, Aunt Rose."

"What about the *A?*"

"Well, I needed to add that—you're my baby girl."

That was his story and he stuck to it—for decades.

I stopped asking Daddy to fess up that he named me after himself many years before he died, only because it linked me to him and I loved that. We didn't have much in common. I was sixty years younger than him, after all.

However, I learned to love my name and everything it represented about my culture, thanks to an article in *Essence* magazine.

Essence is a lifestyle magazine for Black women that was founded in 1970 and is still considered to be a bible for many Black women. A gift subscription to it was part of the rite of passage for many young Black girls, including me.

Although it was predominantly a fashion magazine, showcasing the depth and breadth of Black beauty and talent, it would also feature at least one article about our history and culture in every issue. I always wished more ink was devoted to those types of articles. We were even more starved for media positivity back then, so I guess there has been some progress.

One article made my heart swell with pride. The writer illuminated how many Black folks, especially those raised in the South under Jim Crow, knew that White folks would never willingly address their children with respectful titles such as Mr., Miss, Mrs., Sir, and Madam, even when those children were adults.

I knew that Black folks in general, but especially down South during Jim Crow, were considered the least among humans by White folks—who even memorialize it by counting them as three-fifths of a person during slavery. Still, that attitude was shocking to me.

Addressing adults with respect was so drilled into us as kids that no matter how old I get, my first impulse upon meeting an older Black person is to call them Mr. or Ms. So and So until they tell me otherwise, and even then, tread lightly.

According to the article, some of our ancestors did one of the most powerful things, hidden in plain sight, to protect and love up on their kids. It was something that would give their children an idea that they were, in fact and as indicated by *name*, worthy of respect.

I am not sure if this matter was discussed among parents or if it was something that simply could not be spoken but also could not be contained. Despite the fact that their humanity was so often denied, they subconsciously named their children titles that demanded respect.[1]

That's why my dad was named Major Wade Carter.

Daddy said his hair was gray by the time he was thirty, and it was completely white since my earliest memories of him. He had no lines on his face, but his almond-shaped eyes, narrow nose and lips, and high cheekbones seemed carved into his face, the color of a Hershey's Special Dark chocolate bar.

Daddy was sixty years old when I was born, and up until the very last of his ninety-one years, when he shrank a bit, he was an imposing six foot two and 220 pounds.

As a teenager, when I told friends from school that my dad was in his seventies, they would invariably laugh about how decrepit my ancient father must be. And then they would meet him.

He would look down into their eyes as he reached in for a handshake, enveloping their hand in his huge mitt. And then he would ask how they were doing in school.

He didn't want his daughter hanging out with dummies.

"You said your pops was a senior citizen! That is *not* a seventy-five-year-old man! He could kick my ass. He just dyes his hair white to mess with people. And he was in the Army too, right?"

One of my friends actually called him Major Carter instead of Mr. Carter. Daddy gently told him to call him Mr. Carter, since Major was his given name.

He was in the National Guard during World War II but never ranked, and I don't think he ever thought about messing with anyone, at least not like my friends thought. He was too focused on living out his own version of a life worth living. He was a compulsive gambler, which made life difficult and exciting for the family at times, but you would never find a more personable or curious man.

Born in 1907, just one generation out of slavery in Americus, Georgia, my father started working at the age of thirteen to support his family. He often told me that if things had been a little, or rather a lot, different for him, he would have liked to study law.

He was a huge fan of the legendary lawyer Clarence Darrow, who argued some of the most significant cases of the early twentieth century such as the Scopes "Monkey Trial," which paved the way for evolution to be taught in public schools, and he defended Ossian Sweet and his family, a Black family in Detroit, who were accused of murder after their home was attacked by a White mob.

"Major Wade Carter, Esquire. Woulda had a nice ring to it."

I heard him say that more than once. I agreed.

Both my parents and my older relatives whom I wanted to ask about that naming practice were long dead by the time I saw that article in *Essence*. Regardless, I embraced it and wove it into a narrative of my choosing.

My name was the feminized version of a powerful name that my grandparents, both born into slavery, gave to my father. He was the seventh son of a seventh son.

Seven is not my favorite number—four is, same as Beyoncé! But the number seven is considered significant in many ways. God created the world in seven days. Seven is considered a lucky number. There are seven wonders of the world and seven brides for seven brothers.

So you can see how I make patterns in my head. Don't we all? We are always subconsciously searching for significance in things around us because we are human and want to believe that things that happen to and around us have meaning.

I fantasized that my grandparents' naming their seventh and youngest son Major was their love letter to him. Even if it was done subconsciously, it was an act of subversion within an oppressive system and it showed their resilience and love for their child, reflecting the hope that he would see his own value, even if the world negated it at every turn.

And in turn, my dad's naming me Majora was his love letter to me, his seventh child, his only baby girl, his last messenger going forward. Did he understand that my staking a claim for my own happiness and ambition would be challenged constantly and that I would have to decide how far I was willing to go and how much I was willing to subject myself to obtain them?

Choosing to Not Remember Things Too Painful to Forget

I have no idea if Daddy thought consciously about whether giving me a powerful name would help me see myself as powerful, but I have discovered anecdotally that many Black families either do not know or do not share a great deal about the family history that got them where they are now.

I remember hearing a vague recollection from my Aunt Rose, who lived in the apartment on the top floor of the building I grew up in. Once when I was not even in double digits, she mentioned that when she and her siblings were growing up in Georgia, some of their relatives and friends were "taken up by chain gangs." She described how they were walking through town, minding their own business, arrested for "vagrancy," and then forced by the local White law enforcement to "work off their fines" through hard labor in businesses owned by local White men, such as quarries and mines.

When I asked for more information, she wouldn't directly address my questions. She just changed the subject. Something in her posture made me unwilling to press her for more details.

More than thirty years later, I read Douglas A. Blackmon's Pulitzer Prize–winning book, *Slavery by Another Name: The Re-Enslavement of Black Americans from the Civil War to World War II*. The chain gangs my aunt furtively mentioned were the legal way that the labor of former slaves and their descendants was once again someone else's profit. Even though their freedom had technically been secured by the Emancipation Proclamation, the cruel specter of slavery still had teeth. And it bit hard.

I also learned about these mythical but very, very real places called Black Wall Streets. They were the places where Blacks settled after slavery with housing, banks, schools, and businesses to service them since White communities nearby openly discriminated against them. Some of these places reached such a level of economic success that they attracted the brutal attention of White neighbors who literally destroyed them overnight—savagely and without consequence.

The most famous of them is the town of Greenwood in Tulsa, Oklahoma. Immortalized in many documentaries and used as the setting in the HBO series *Watchmen* and *Lovecraft Country*, Greenwood was the epicenter of the 1921 massacre, incited by a false report that a White woman was assaulted by a Black man.

Within less than twenty-five hours, between one hundred and three hundred people were killed, approximately fifteen hundred buildings were burned or looted across thirty-five acres, and more than eight thousand of the ten thousand Black people living there were rendered homeless without recourse.[2]

Some residents stayed and tried rebuilding what was lost. The Black community of Greenwood is still struggling today. Laboriously but steadily over the years, they were able to rebuild some of what was lost, but a highway construction project dismantled that work in the 1960s and now fewer than forty businesses in the Greenwood area are Black owned.[3]

I wonder what happened to the people who lived through the riots and settled somewhere else in the country—what we would call internally displaced persons today.

Although the actual riot was scrubbed from historical accounts for decades, those in Black communities around the country heard about it and felt its chill. This was recently substantiated by economist Lisa Cook, who cross-referenced the sizable decrease in the numbers of US Patent Office filings by Black people after Tulsa.[4] When it was demonstrated even into the twenty-first century that White mob savagery would be excused or supported without question by the state, why bother expecting protection at any level?

I can't imagine the level of post-traumatic stress they must have felt. What reason did they offer to others about why they showed up in another town from Greenwood to rebuild their lives? Did they share accounts as a cautionary tale, or did they feel like they could not talk too much about it even in the company of those they trusted intimately like my Aunt Rose did with me that one and only time?

Dream Management

Maybe my aunts and my dad felt instinctively that they should not get their hopes too high about anyone's future. Dreaming too big often led to disappointment.

Yes, we could grow up and be anything we put our minds to, but we had to be careful because it could all be burned overnight. Such is the fate of being born Black in America.

In the months before my dad died in 1999, he was weak and his balance was off but he was as sharp as ever. At the time, I lived in the house across the street from the house I grew up in. I was squatting in an abandoned but very livable property. It was the 1990s and gentrification was but a whisper in the distance.

I would visit my parents every day to help my mom take care of my dad. He had lost a lot of weight, but he was still 180 pounds of deadweight, and my mom could not handle cleaning, bathing, and feeding him by herself.

I didn't mind though. I didn't have much of a relationship with my dad before he was bedridden, and I thought it would be good to get to know him.

Don't get me wrong. He wasn't a bad guy. He was super interesting, with stories for days. He lived through two world wars, the Great Depression, and the Jim Crow South. He traveled all over the United States and some of Canada and even Mexico as a Pullman porter and a truck driver. He was always on the go and traveled more than most White people of his era.

However, I never felt like one of his favored children. I was the youngest, and part of me thought that since there were so many others and I was definitely the quiet one, he just didn't have cause to notice me much.

But now I was the only kid showing up to feed him and clean him and his bedpans. We got to know each other like never before.

I spent a lot of evenings hanging out with my dad while my mom slept off the stress and physical exhaustion of caring for a husband who just a year before was driving and doing home improvement projects. And I use the term "home improvement" loosely. Daddy was a terrible handyman.

During our evening talks, I would tell Daddy about the work I was doing at a local nonprofit. I had carved out a role for myself there as an environmental justice advocate.

I had discovered an abandoned street that dead-ended at the Bronx River. It was supposed to have been a bridgehead for a highway that was never built, and the dead-end street had been used as an illegal dump for thirty years (figure 3).

We had received a $10,000 seed grant to help restore our part of the Bronx River watershed, an amount that was leveraged many times over. Learning that I could spearhead the transformation of a dump into a park emboldened me. I wanted to use the project as a counterbalance against plans our city and state governments had to build a huge waste facility on our waterfront. I saw it as the physical manifestation of why our city and state governments and even our own community should not view Hunts Point as the repository for all the noxious uses that wealthier and Whiter communities could afford to avoid.

FIGURE 3: Hunts Point Riverside Park, 1998

This was 1997, long before any of the cleanup, design, or events such as community boating, outdoor movie screenings, or music performances had happened. Hunts Point's future was just a gleam in my eye.

One night, I told Daddy all about my own dreams for that dumpy little street end. It would be a place for community, beautiful and green. There would be a pier for launching canoes in the water and for people to fish from. It would announce so much promise that people would see their own beauty reflected in it and it would inspire them to think about what else we could build and do. The possibilities seemed endless to me!

My dad looked at me and smiled gently. He let out a long sigh.

"That sounds bee-u-ti-ful, baby. Jus' bee-u-ti-ful! You think they gonna let my gal do something like that down there? You know White folks don't like us getting too many bee-u-ti-ful things in places like 'round here."

"I'm already working on it, Pop. It doesn't look like much now— it's still a dump—but I can't wait for you to see it when I'm done."

"Ohhweee! I cain't wait to see it—God willing!"

I believe that his initial reticence was rooted in not wanting to have me be disappointed by what invariably happens to so many Black folks that dream above the station afforded to them by the dominant power structure. I know he was just trying to protect me. But still, he knew to throw up a prayer, tentative though it might be.

I was able to spearhead that transformation for a public space that would win a national award for excellence in urban design in 2009 (figure 4).[5]

My dad didn't live to see any of it, but I know he sees it now and knows that his baby girl was responsible for it.

FIGURE 4: Hunts Point Riverside Park, 2006

CHAPTER 6

CONVENIENT PREY

If You're Not at the Table, You're on the Menu

L et's be clear: just because many residents in low-status communities do not see the value within their own community doesn't mean it isn't there. Others definitely see it. An entire industry banks, literally, on the current inhabitants in those communities not recognizing the value.

Predatory speculators are the invasive species in our monoculture metaphor. They prey on those who have been generationally conditioned to believe that their communities have no real value while people like themselves live there. People who feel that way are not wrong. In addition to the period when Black people were considered financeable property in America, land and financing have been systematically denied to people of color over many decades, including the one in which this book is being written (and probably for at least a few more after). We know this because almost all the people responsible for federal and state policy, as well as those leading the banking and real estate industries, wrote down exactly what their intentions were and how they were going to accomplish them.

The current and innocuous-seeming weapons of choice for predatory speculators are to send a mail solicitation (figures 5 and 6), make

FIGURE 5: Home solicitation "offer" A

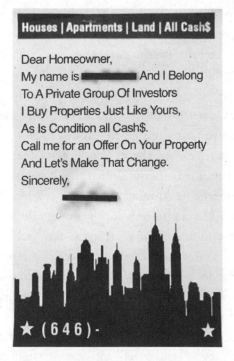

FIGURE 6: Home solicitation "offer" B

a phone call, comb probate court filings for the passage of assets to heirs, or visit property owners' home in low-status communities—with an offer to buy the deed for cash, closing in less than a week. The promise of fast cash for a property in a seemingly valueless community is seductive.

I know this firsthand.

After my parents passed away, I didn't understand that what my siblings and I were about to go through was part of a time-honored tradition of separating people in low-status communities from assets that could have supported generational wealth.

Prior to that, my goal in acquiring my first property was to have a place to live that wasn't in a spare bedroom of Mommy and Daddy's house.

I had zero desire to be some kind of real estate mogul and had no real understanding of either the power of wealth building through real estate or the concurrent history of systemic racism and structural inequality that Ta-Nehisi Coates illustrates so clearly in his seminal article, "The Case for Reparations."[1] I just wanted a place to live away from the prying eyes of my parents.

In hindsight, I now recognize that by taking a second look at our own low-status communities, we can recognize the inherent value within them and how they can help us realize the aspirations for our own lives. Not everyone is going to be able to participate in homeownership at the same level at the same time, and that's okay. When some of us succeed and stay, many more can follow.

My own experiences with predatory speculators range from the incredulous to the tragically sad. I stumbled into homeownership. My family just walked away from it.

The first property I purchased was across the street from the house I grew up in. It once belonged to Miss Odessa Stratford. She was an elderly woman, and as a child, I thought she was rich. She owned her own home, never had a job as far as I could tell, and had traveled the world. I have a vague recollection of her travel photos; one that stood out to me was a black-and-white photo of her walking through the ruins of an Egyptian or Roman temple. She was wearing white gloves and a cloche hat and clasped a tiny purse with both of her hands. The upturned corners of her huge smile nearly touched the bottom of her rhinestone-edged cat's-eye glasses. She was a woman clearly satisfied with life in general.

My mother was very close to Miss Stratford, who was like her second mother.

When Miss Stratford fell ill in the early 1980s, she was barely able to leave her home, let alone travel. My parents took over her care. My mother would make dinner for our family and then walk across the street to take a plate of food to Miss Stratford and spend a little time with her before coming back to us. She collected rent from Miss Stratford's tenants and made sure the electric and oil bills were paid. My dad took care of repairs as needed.

One day, while helping my mom clean Miss Stratford's house, I overheard her Miss Stratford say to my mom, "Tinnie, I need to change my will. My family doesn't care about this house—maybe not me either. I need to leave this house to you."

My mother demurred, saying something about how her family must care for her—they just must be very busy with their own lives. My mom assured her that she would always be there to take care of her anyway and that she wasn't worried about the house. She just wanted Miss Stratford to get better.

Miss Stratford sucked her teeth and said, "I need to remember to call my lawyer."

I don't think she ever did.

She died a few years later. I don't recall ever meeting any members of her family. I just knew she had a brother with a memorable name whom she spoke of without details but with loads of contempt.

At one point, Miss Stratford had been dead for over a decade, and no one in her family had ever come to check in on the house. My parents still took care of the building. My favorite uncle, my mother's younger brother, Levi, moved into one of the apartments, and my sister and her family moved into Miss Stratford's former apartment, which helped pay the bills on the house, especially after Miss Stratford's tenants stopped paying rent and then moved out in the middle of the night.

Around that time, I had returned to the neighborhood and had been living in my parents' house for about a year and desperately wanted a place of my own. I took up residence in the apartment that Miss Stratford's tenants abandoned. Some friends and I spent weeks ripping out old 1970s-era shag carpeting and mirrored wall tiles and painting the apartment a kaleidoscope of jewel tones.

When I asked my dad who owned the house, he said nobody. Miss Stratford's will had never been executed, but he thought our family would eventually secure the deed. He wanted my siblings to take the lead, but they weren't interested in living in or owning property in the neighborhood. He suggested I should try and get the deed. I had already started working in community development within the neighborhood, so it seemed like I might be there for a while. I decided to lay down some roots and stabilize my housing situation.

I found a lawyer and borrowed enough money to pay him. He filed a claim on the house in probate court and was giddy about arguing an *adverse possession* case, in which he would assert that I was the rightful owner since my possession of the house was "open and hostile." This was very exciting and new to both of us.

My lawyer made a token offer on my behalf to the closest heir in Miss Stratford's will. Within days after the papers were delivered, the *New York Times* published an article about how the South Bronx was the next frontier for real estate development in New York City, and the photo used in the article was of my block!

The surviving family members became aware of the changing circumstances of the house they once ignored utterly, and now they wanted above full market value for it. That wasn't going to happen. They had walked away from the house and we did take care of it for many years.

Within days of determining that we would pursue a court case, I received a call from a man claiming that he was the new owner of my building and that he needed to meet with me and the other tenants. He told me that he'd purchased it from Miss Stratford's brother, the same one she held in deep contempt, as evidenced by language in her will.

After leaving tens of thousands of dollars to all the other heirs, she concluded her will with these words: "And to my brother _____, I leave the sum of $25.00 for reasons best left between him and me."

The supposed new owner obtained a fraudulent deed in cahoots with Miss Stratford's specious brother, emboldening the new owner to try to evict me in landlord-tenant court. I had to bear the indignity of watching the opposing lawyers and the judge for the case laugh and joke with each other, while the judge callously snapped at me and other defendants. There was an uncomfortably cozy relationship between real estate interests and the judiciary that I am sure I was not the first to experience. It looked like I could lose the house right there.

However, because my lawyer had staked a claim on the house for me early on, I was able to pursue a path to legitimately acquire that house. It took two agonizing years, but I closed on my house the day before Thanksgiving in 2004. The word "grateful" took on a depth I could not fathom until then.

I hosted Thanksgiving that year with my mother at the head of the table, and my future husband, James, made a feast with different kinds of birds: a pheasant, a goose, and a duck. No turkeys were allowed in my home; I'd had enough of them. It was quite a celebration.

A few weeks later, I received a call from Miss Stratford's creepy little brother, congratulating me on getting the house. I told him Miss Stratford was right about him and hung up the phone.

My own mother died the next year, and I was unable to persuade my siblings to hold on to our family's home—just across the street from Miss Stratford's. My siblings appreciated my efforts to revitalize their old neighborhood, but none of them felt any interest in keeping our family's property.

I was unaware of the steady loss of Black-owned land nationally, and my thinking was still a long way off from what later evolved into my approach to community development. But after everything I had put myself through to acquire the property that our family had invested in over those years, I felt strongly that we should keep our family home in the family. I was horrified to realize that everyone else was fine with liquidating our family's asset in a rapidly appreciating real estate market—erasing hope for the next generation to accumulate that wealth from their parents.

The house was quickly sold to a holding company in 2005 for about $300,000. After satisfying the mortgage and paying the lawyer, taxes, surcharges, and fees, less than $100,000 remained to be split among seven heirs.

In the early 2020s, the house that my dad bought in the 1940s for $15,000 was valued at more than forty-five times his initial investment. That's more than $700,000 on the balance sheet of some holding company and not my family's balance sheet. When you hear about the yawning Black wealth gap in America, this is a part of how it is happening: real estate liquidation.

In addition to the historical and well-documented issues regarding the lack of access to capital and other heinous forms of housing discrimination directed at Black Americans by every level of government as well as the banking and real estate industries, many of us lacked basic real estate acumen and thus have sold or refinanced in ways that come back to bite us later in the form of unrealized benefits for our own families. And yes, the type of outright fraud as was attempted on Miss Stratford's estate is not uncommon.

The already diminished amount of property in the hands of Black Americans is evaporating rapidly. This means more and more renters, fewer owners, and a reduced ability to leverage assets for our own future well-being.

My family's story is not unique.

Black and Latino families that were able to purchase property during the era of White flight are selling early and cheap at the same time that reurbanization is causing land values to appreciate dramatically.[2] These families can be seen as relatively unsophisticated "investors" who make six-figure transactions with no requirement for counsel or protection—something the federal Securities and Exchange Commission would not allow in other investment scenarios. They often sell below market for cash deals when families who could afford a mortgage are searching nearby. The sellers fall out of potential wealth building, and rarely, if ever, get back in. Other nearby willing and financially able minority families can't even get to the gate because speculators beat them to it.

The predatory speculators are always looking for a way in and are banking on folks not seeing the potential value of their own communities.

Reurbanization means that migratory patterns are shifting back to cities. Baby boomers and millennials are competing for the same walkable, transit rich, and architecturally appealing spaces.[3]

Additionally, current housing construction is simply not meeting the demand for housing types affordable to people with a range of incomes.

With all that, I am left with some uncomfortable questions:

+ What happens once the prey is fed upon?
+ Why is there prey anyway?
+ Is there another way to do real estate development?

CHAPTER 7

WHY MUST WE DO REAL ESTATE DEVELOPMENT THE SAME OLD WAY?

My company identified two types of real estate development that happen in American low-status communities as a result of reurbanization.

One is commonly referred to as "gentrification," and it appears that current residents are being displaced because they are either priced out of rentals or they sell before the neighborhood changes. Neither group reaps the benefits of being in neighborhoods that experience an improved quality of life while the residents are in it.

The other type is what my company calls "poverty-level economic maintenance" (PLEM), where many successful economic engines are in play, but little to none of the economic activity generated benefits residents in the community. Furthermore, the vernacular of PLEM communities shares attributes with common built environments.

And I am aware that the acronym PLEM sounds and looks like "phlegm." There's nothing attractive about either term. For example,

+ Low-status communities do not have diverse food options. Chances are fast-food chains will be much easier to find than healthy, good quality produce in supermarkets or farmers markets.

+ Instead of banks, credit unions, or investment clubs that can help you grow your money, you'll find check-cashing stores,

payday loan spots, pawn shops, and rent-to-own stores, all of
which charge a premium for you to access your own money.

+   Dollar stores and other low-grade retail options often make
    people feel the need to travel outside their own community to
    spend their money.

+   The multibillion-dollar pharmaceutical industry does very
    well treating the lifestyle-related health conditions that plague
    low-status communities, including diabetes, obesity, and
    heart conditions.

+   In tacit support of the pharmaceutical industry are the
    government-subsidized health clinics writing the prescriptions
    that treat the symptoms of all lifestyle-related conditions.

+   A commercial option for self-medication is readily available,
    and I don't mean yoga studios or health food stores. Liquor
    stores dot the landscape at regular intervals.

+   And last but definitely not least, these communities have a
    disproportionate amount of subsidized housing for very
    low-income people and homeless shelters.

One can argue a chicken-or-the-egg scenario regarding whether
poverty attracts these commercial activities or these businesses attract
poverty, but the net result is continued, persistent, generational, concentrated poverty. And with concentrated poverty, statistically, the
negative conditions we all want to see alleviated get exacerbated: poor
health outcomes, low educational attainment, higher rates of families that have a family member in the criminal justice system, higher
unemployment, and of course, higher poverty rates. They combine to
metastasize a pernicious lack of hope in the future of the community.

It is hard to argue with anyone who would want to leave a place like
that if they had the opportunity to do so. However, I did wonder why
we have only these two kinds of real estate development in low-status
communities: one designed to actively exclude people from projects
that could have benefited them, the other designed to make them suffer.

Gentrification doesn't start when you see middle-class White
people, cute cafes, and doggie daycares in formerly poor communities

of color or even when predatory speculators smell the blood of an easy victim. It starts when people in low-status communities believe that there is no value there. On economic, spiritual, and emotional levels, it is not uncommon for many of us born and raised in low-status communities to disengage from them instead of building them up.

That leaves entire communities open for predation and vulnerable to the systems and policies that created the wealth gap between White Americans and Black Americans and other people of color in our country. It reduces opportunities for wealth creation through real estate ownership and business development that is a cornerstone of White American success but has been systematically denied to communities of color for centuries. However, by stemming the loss of appreciable assets held in the hands of communities of color, we can help close an ever-widening wealth gap.

I believe that community is not just a place; it's an activity. We also need the infrastructure that allows community-building activity to occur.

I have seen and experienced the trauma and drama of the generational impacts of concentrated poverty within my own community, and even my own family, and I believe that we need to promote more economic diversity starting from the inside out. Everything we know about biodiversity applies to the economic ecosystem that governs the built environment of low-status communities.

It's like putting oysters back in a struggling river. They are not the biggest part of the ecosystem, but they provide a crucial service by helping to clean the waterways, which helps support the conditions of all the other life around them.

Creating a Culture of Reinvestment from the Inside

The value of *talent retention* to companies and the detriment of *brain drain* to developing economies are well known and documented.

In low-status American communities, success is often measured by how far one gets away, leaving the door open for those with less sensitivity to neighborhood development. How can we draw more local talent to stay in place, spend, and thrive as well as welcome new capital sources to build on their example? A successful long-term approach to community development involves at its foundation a talent-retention strategy.

First, we need to acknowledge that we have never had a shortage of talented people emerging from our low-status communities and that collectively, we set up the conditions for their exodus.

I want to create opportunities that make people feel as though their community is something that they want to be in and stay in. That is a hard task.

I engage with people in low-status communities around the country. Many share that their communities have a multitude of issues that they don't like. However, they are the devil they know, and if and when they see change, especially if it is considered positive change, they report feeling that it could not possibly include them.

When you disrupt any kind of system, you will get resistance; some might be out of curiosity or fear, and some might even be destructive. But if you stay in it for the long haul, you show not only that you are conscious that change can be hard but also how you can flow with it so it connects to something that could work for our communities

+ If we demystify the way the housing market and development actually work and consider participating ourselves
+ If we can help build our credit
+ If we can help others understand the value of retaining ownership in our family's home instead of selling it to a predatory speculator
+ If we could think about local business development and marshal existing resources to do it sustainably

I could go on, but that's what the rest of the book is for. I believe that a talent-retention approach applied to development in low-status communities will create healthier ecosystems and show people that you don't have to move out of your neighborhood to live in a better one.

Minority Americans have been openly discriminated against in terms of access to capital and access to the development of their own communities. I am impatient about creating opportunities for social and racial equality. I use a talent-retention real estate development strategy as a tool, and I am confident that it will be more effective in the long run than the status quo.

We saw the problem of status quo development and as part of my practice, I don't presume much, I launch ideas in context. I want to broaden the idea of who should do development and expand an approach that creates reasons for emotional and economic wealth creation in low-status communities, designed to retain talent, and not repel it.

CHAPTER 8

SUCCESS DOESN'T LIVE
AROUND HERE FOR LONG

Whenever we describe an economic sector in front of the words "industrial complex," we are usually focusing on the conflict of interest generated by its parts benefiting from finding ever more problems to address, as opposed to coming to a fruitful solution. For example, President Eisenhower warned of the military industrial complex on his way out of office. As the former Supreme Allied Commander in World War II, he understood that the manufacture of weapons created a dependency on its jobs and economic activity and would inspire others to produce and deploy similar weapons, increasing our risk, demanding more weapons to address the risk, and so on.

Within the nonprofit industrial complex, I have observed an epidemic level of what I call "goal dysmorphia," where the stated goals, such as equality, uplift, self-actualization, and triumph over big obstacles, are not only never fully achieved but undermined by a pervasive mindset that treats the symptoms but does not cure the disease, thereby entrenching constant need and more nonprofit activity, thus, an industrial complex.

A nonprofit industrial complex model is attracted to sources of despair, so these sources are reflexively sheltered from actual change and viewed as a resource, and customer base, if you will. It spawns

an echo chamber that spans the social justice, philanthropic, government, and academic sectors. The complex benefits, grows, hires more
of its friends, spends even more money to perpetuate itself, persuades
universities to recognize nonprofit management majors, holds conferences in fun cities, and on and on. Yet nearly all of the problems it
claims to address don't get any better and most often get worse.

It recognizes and validates only those that fit a profile of perpetual
need. In this model, the lack of interest in supporting homegrown
talent to facilitate change from within should come as no surprise.

You Don't Belong in This Club

When my star started to rise as an example of leadership and strategy out of left field, I was seen as an "inspiring" figure. However, the
results of my efforts, which showed an effective but different way of
supporting low-status communities, were not taken seriously by the
nonprofit industrial complex.

Indeed, billions of dollars have been spent on philanthropic and
public programs that are designed to provide direct services to folks
rather than *invest* in their future financial development. A case in
point was the enthusiasm generated by the green jobs movement in
the mid-2000s.

I listened to the contenders for the Democratic nomination for
president in 2008. Barack Obama, Hillary Clinton, and John Edwards
all trumpeted the importance of green jobs during their debate. My
heart swelled with pride and hope for our country's future. The work
of the organization I founded and led at that time, Sustainable South
Bronx (SSBx), had played a large role in creating that buzz.

Our signature project was a green job training program and placement system. In addition to training, we focused on ensuring that our
graduates had living-wage jobs after they graduated. To be a part of
the solution, we engaged the problem. In this case, it meant forming
human relationships with employers to really learn about who and
what they were looking to hire, when, and why—enabling us to help

support those businesses (a little industrial complex of our own, I guess).

We put an emphasis on researching the jobs that were currently available and worked with potential employers to ensure that our trainees were well-qualified as well as well-suited for the job market and the companies we wanted to see grow. We also provided support for the trainees even after they left our program and entered the workforce, just to make sure they were adjusting well. A less than 50 percent placement rate was common in many job training programs, but our trainees benefited from an 85 percent placement rate.

We conducted market research and discovered that we could create our own enterprise to directly employ some of our trainees. We started a green and cool roof installation business and funneled profits back into operations for the training program.

Another part of SSBx worked on advocacy that could directly impact the future job market. For example, we cofounded and coled the SWIM (Stormwater Infrastructure Matters) Coalition. Convening more than fifty diverse agencies to strategize around New York City's long-term pollution control plan, we successfully advocated for and achieved policies and legislation that supported job-creation vehicles such as a tax abatement for green roof installations, a growing industry and job creator.

Before and during Obama's first term in the White House, many very well-funded green job *training* programs were established all over the country. However, despite the model that we presented, very little attention was paid to promoting policies and new business development that would hire those trainees once they graduated from those programs.

There were, of course, wonderful and notable outliers to that job-training-only paradigm. One was Detroiters Working for Environmental Justice. Back in those days, the organization was run by a fierce, funny woman named Donele Wilkins. I was delighted to learn how the group incorporated the same kind of strategies that we used and got even better results than we did—a 90 percent placement rate!

Although I am very proud of the work that we accomplished, my heart still aches because I was unable to convince my peers or higher-ups in positions that could have advanced local or national policy to champion sustainable business development with accessible job creation, in addition to advocacy. From where I stood, funds were spent primarily on green job training programs, with very little focus on where the jobs actually were or could come from, how to get them, and to whom which jobs were actually going to be available.

By focusing on green job training without addressing placement challenges and opportunities, the green jobs movement fizzled, becoming an also-ran before the end of Obama's first term. In the communities where people needed those green jobs, the nonprofit industrial complex and policymakers had successfully maintained the status quo.

The Status Quo: Poverty as a Cultural Attribute

Why was so much more attention and funding applied to training than to creating the policy or infrastructure to produce actual jobs? Why is it that so much is spent on philanthropic and government programs designed to eradicate poverty and all its attendant issues yet the statistics stay the same?

Please note, I am not ignoring the roles that systemic racism and our caste system play in why this country is plagued with poverty, low educational attainment, and poor health outcomes, among other issues, in low-status communities. What I am suggesting is that the default reasoning of the nonprofit industrial complex is that *poverty is the culture* of low-status communities;[1] and thus, it will forever be linked to those communities in a way that demands more nonprofit attention.

Brain drain is the cousin of the poverty-as-culture dynamic. Those who seemingly have more hope for their future—for example, the ones who excel in school or are physically or artistically gifted—are encouraged to leave and seek their fortunes elsewhere. Thus, poverty levels are maintained because those who show early promise to "rise above" that station go on to measure their success by how far away they get from their own communities. We are meant to see our exceptionalism as a gift that we then export for the benefit of ourselves and others outside of our hometown. The inference is that those remaining in these communities should be provided with tools to tolerate their poverty—and again feed the complex.

So is poverty a cultural attribute—something forever entrenched within those communities and by extension equated with neighborhood preservation? Is that why the ones who can probably make it out are identified early and constantly supplied reasons to measure success by how far away they get from their own hometown?

Let Us Show You the Way Out

Many community-based organizations expound the principles of "asset-based community development," which translates to seeing the community itself as an asset. Yet despite that laudable phrase, it seems to me that most of their programs are designed with the expectation that the talented residents will eventually leave for greener pastures (brain drain) and the people who stay are destined for persistent poverty, so they need programs to "help" them (such as advocacy for affordable rental housing for the lowest income people and homeless shelters).

"Bright" students are directed into "gifted and talented" classes and provided with tutoring and programs designed to steer them toward college or employment. In essence, they are being shepherded out of the neighborhood.

It is assumed that they will grow up and get out of the hood. Perhaps they will eventually "give back" in some way once they become successful. However, that is not required or expected.

At three years old, I was deemed one of the bright ones. I distinctly remember reading all my birthday cards out loud to my mother on my fourth birthday and sitting on my dad's lap to read him articles from the newspaper that interested me.

Education is often hailed by community leaders, government officials, and political pundits as the solution to erase the stain of growing up in a neighborhood that was deemed less-than by popular culture. Communities like mine have an inferiority complex steeped into them.

It is painful to admit that I bought into the idea that nothing good would *stay* good if it stayed in my neighborhood. It has been a process for me to understand how deliberately that concept is perpetuated and reinforced through various channels, politically and culturally, despite the fact that neighborhoods like the South Bronx, just like any other neighborhood, produce people with a beautiful and diverse array of talents.

It has proven to be an even more difficult and nuanced concept to communicate in a system that generally maintains that poverty is ingrained in the very fabric of the life of a low-status community. And it is why I push so hard to overcome that dynamic.

We See You—Sort Of

I spent many years as an environmental advocate in my hometown. Through Sustainable South Bronx, the project-based environmental solutions organization that I founded and led from 2001–2008, I pioneered the green job training and placement systems that gave folks from my community, including some ex-offenders and many who were on public assistance, both a personal and financial stake in restoring their community. I spearheaded the development of a national-award-winning park project and launched a green-roofing business under it as well.

All that and more caught the attention of the MacArthur Foundation, and I was endowed with one of its unofficially named "genius" awards in 2005. I delivered a TED Talk that was one of the first six released online—and just a few months after the MacArthur announcement put me in an international spotlight. Since then, I've been a sought-after speaker at conferences all over the world.

Despite all that I had accomplished, I knew I was missing something. Exactly what, I wasn't sure, but I knew that the environmental abuses that my community had been targeted to tolerate were just the tip of the iceberg. The underlying problems came from someplace deeper and even more dangerous to our well-being.

Slowly, I was forming the basis of the thesis that would later become central to my thinking about community development: *retaining the talent that was born and raised in low-status communities could be a key to these communities' economic recovery.* Concurrently, the proverbial light bulb went on over my head, and I knew my time within the nonprofit industrial complex was coming to an end.

I left SSBx in 2008, at least three years later than I should have. I had "reverse founder syndrome." I had set a firm foundation and I knew the organization would be fine, it was me I was worried about.

I loved my work and I had a great, hardworking team, but being the visionary leader of an oxymoron—an internationally renowned nontraditional grassroots environmental organization—*and* being a Black woman was just too much for the philanthropic world to wrap its paternalistic little mind around.

The more attention I received, the harder I had to work for funding, which ultimately did not materialize. We had a few funders that stuck by me throughout it all, but then there were the others.

More than a few potential funders told me in the same breath that they wouldn't support my organization and that it shouldn't be too hard for me to find funding, but they offered no assistance or guidance. I even had one of them request a full day of my time *for free* to tour their board *after* they turned me down flat for funding. The nerve.

One foundation promised a capacity-building grant that I would've used to plan my organization's next phase but pulled it at the last minute with the excuse that we would be fine without its money and that another group that was not as "well known" or as "effective" as mine needed it more.

I was prominently featured in and even the cover girl of philanthropic publications, like the discontinued *Contribute* magazine, which had me posed literally shoulder to shoulder with then Citibank CEO Sandy Weill as if we were part of the same club. Although I am sure I provided all those publications with great content, I cannot point to any benefit my organization derived from the association.

One consortium of extremely well-endowed philanthropists wanted me to spend two days with them to advise them at their retreat because historically they never heard from people of color at their retreats. When I asked about compensation, they told me that "philosophically," they did not offer compensation but assured me that the engagement would raise my profile as a sustainability leader. I reminded them that they came to me because they already knew I was a leader.

I asked another very well-regarded philanthropic leader if they would use their connections to introduce me to people who could help me build up my board into a fundraising one. They told me point-blank that they didn't know anyone who would be interested in joining my board.

Years later, I watched as that same very well-regarded philanthropic leader gave a cheeky talk about supporting an organization led by a white woman and giving her a grant three times as large as what she had asked for because they felt she didn't ask for enough. Ironically enough, much of the work her organization did was to report on the importance of work like mine.

I did call that philanthropic leader on their double standard. I hold no ill will toward that White lady. She was just doing her thing, and that philanthropic leader was doing what had always been done in their industry: devaluing homegrown talent.

I could go on and on, with more reports of the major and minor indignities that come with the territory of being a Black woman in America comfortable with asserting herself, but I'll cut to the chase. Philanthropy has never favored organizations led by people of color.[2]

I sat in the audience of the 2007 TED conference listening to Isabel Allende discussing creativity and feminism. She said, "The poorest and most backward societies are always those that put women down. Yet this obvious truth is ignored by governments and also by philanthropy. For every dollar given to a women's program, 20 dollars are given to men's programs."[3]

I sat there with silent tears streaming down my face. My husband sat beside me, gently stroking my arm. I'd spent much of the past year or so taking paid speaking engagements at conferences all over the world to cover the shortfall in my agency's budget.

My philanthropic support had been steadily drying up as the expectations of an organization led by a MacArthur-winning, TED-talking grassroots visionary were growing daily. All those speaking engagements eventually filled the $300,000 gap in my budget so we could continue operating at the level we needed to, but it was at a huge cost to my well-being.

The title of a legendary feminist anthology in Black women's studies, *All the Women Are White, All the Blacks Are Men, but Some of Us Are Brave*, rang through my head as Isabel spoke. I had received bitter validation that I was doomed to fail if I left myself at the mercy of the philanthropic sector.

Note to Self: Don't Try to Be a Part of Any Club That Doesn't Want You as a Member

Although I was ultimately successful in parlaying my speaking engagements to cover the shortfall in my budget, the stress of trying to support my organization had taken a toll on me. I was chronically tired and had gained nearly thirty pounds in less than a year.

I had been hospitalized twice during my career in community development, which was less than a decade old at the time. The first time, in the late 1990s, I pushed through fever, aches and pains, and welts that materialized on my body, signs that my body was valiantly trying to fight off an infection.

Why would I do that? I had an event to coordinate, Represent the Reel: The South Bronx Film & Video Festival. No, I wasn't trying to promote examples of "poverty porn," showcasing how degraded and in need of help my community was. This wasn't a social service festival. I saw it as a celebration highlighting the cinematic talent of the South Bronx, as well as national and international filmmakers.

I missed the opening night because I was in the hospital strapped to an IV with antibiotics treating a kidney infection gone amok.

The second time was during the planning of an event to reactivate a site along the Bronx River as a community asset. At the time, the former concrete plant was home to abandoned ancient silos filled with hardened concrete and an old shed that served as a residence for a homeless family. The family eventually found permanent and much more humane housing, but community groups like ours wanted to introduce the site of the former concrete plant as part of the future of the greenway along the Bronx River.

During the planning, once again I ignored the signs that something was wrong in my body. I had developed a pain in my neck that wouldn't go away for weeks, and I felt I had too much to do to take the time to see a doctor. Warm compresses made the pain manageable.

I traveled to meetings around the city with a microwavable herb-filled heating pad. Before a meeting started, I'd ask to use the office microwave and participate in the meeting with my heating pad draped around my neck, smelling like rosemary.

Turns out, three disks in my neck were herniated. The pain became unbearable, and finally I was put in a South Bronx hospital that took advantage of my health insurance by keeping me there drugged out on a morphine, valium, and codeine diet for two weeks.

Because of all the "pain management," I was blitzed out of my mind and could not advocate for myself. Two of my besties for life, Janine Simon Daughtry, my friend since high school, and Hugh Hogan, a newer colleague turned friend, met while visiting me at the hospital and figured out how to get me into another hospital where I was administered a steroid treatment and sent home within two days.

Obviously, I missed the event I was planning at the time as well.

All that to say, the thirty extra pounds of stress I was carrying after running myself around the world to support my organization was weighing on me, pun intended. I was grateful to have a dedicated and talented team at work, but mine was a grueling job: constantly working behind the scenes to sustain our incredible work, knowing that the philanthropic world claimed me publicly as one of its golden ones but treated me like a stepchild.

It took me many, many months after hearing Isabel Allende's words to finally make the decision to save my own life by leaving SSBx. It happened while I was participating in a retreat for social justice leaders called Rockwood Leadership Institute. The sessions were led by master facilitators Robert Gass and Jodie Tonita. One particular session was a healing circle, led by Rachel Bagby, an acclaimed cultural change advisor. When she sang a sacred song, something inside me broke open.

First, tears of relief flowed as I recognized and then released the pain I carried. Then I broke into a joyful dance as I gleefully ran around the room belting out a running verse something like "I hate being an executive director and I don't have to do it anymore!" What would we do without an occasional earthy-crunchy retreat?

Despite barely being able to contain myself as I thought of my liberation, there was no way I was going to do anything except prepare for a graceful transition. I wanted to ensure that we had an exit strategy that would cause the least disruption to the staff and their work.

I hired my friend Kelly McGowan, an acclaimed organizational strategy consultant, and she worked with the board of directors, the staff, and me to come up with a plan. The plan we devised was a year-long process that involved keeping me on part-time as support to an interim executive director who would handle operations while the new executive director search went on later in the year.

The board was clearly just humoring me and had already started on other plans. I was literally sitting at the table when they started discussing retaining the Majora Carter "brand" as if I wasn't even in the room. They seemed completely surprised, offended even, when I told them that only I would be handling my brand, although I would be inclined to use it for the organization—within limits I defined.

Many of the philanthropic organizations that turned me down when I led the organization rushed in to support it after I left. The board boasted that the $300,000 gap that my departure represented was filled within months.

My board also decided to immediately hire my deputy director as the new executive director, raising their new salary to greater than $25,000 more than mine had been. The new director's approach to their new position became so contrary to the mission of the organization that the staff started a union to protect themselves and the organization. When the board chair asked me to help them with the issue, I strongly suggested supporting the staff, accepting unionization with open arms, and curtailing the executive director's "leadership" approach in an attempt to try to bridge the divide that had developed between them and the staff.

The response of the board was to remove my name from the organization's website as founder and fire the two staffers they recognized as the union's main organizers. It was their loss all around, and the entire experience just validated that the nonprofit industrial complex was not set up to support organically grown, homegrown leaders like me.

Sure, I could have fought to stay involved with SSBx but why? It was clear that my board of directors as well as the nonprofit industry in general only saw me as an asset to exploit.

I was a *special* one, a MacArthur Fellow, a TED speaker. They seemed to revel in their association with my accomplishments, but ultimately, I felt like they saw me as the featured performer in the sustainability minstrel show, but they were not into my acting all uppity. For example, I was disgusted but not surprised when a 2020 study conducted by researchers at the Tishman Environment and Design Center at the New School showed that large philanthropic organizations gave nearly 99 percent of their US climate funding to White-led groups with just 1.3 percent going to Black, Indigenous, and other people of color—led environmental justice groups that were doing the most to fight climate change within their own communities.[4] That study and others were all I needed to validate my belief that those of us who sought to work to support our own communities were categorically denied the opportunity to do so effectively.

I think it is yet another one of the insidious byproducts of the effectiveness of the White supremacist message that is ingrained in American culture: Black folks are not meant to be trusted. Not with money. Not even with their own lives. And *especially* not if they are using their lives and money in service of others like them.

CHAPTER 9

IF THEY DON'T SEE IT, THEY WON'T BELIEVE IT

I remember when Jimmy Carter, then a presidential candidate, came to visit the South Bronx. We didn't go to meet him, but my family was all atwitter about it since he was a Carter too, just like us!

We talked about his visit at the dinner table. My mom said, "Seems like a nice man, but nothing around here will change." My father nodded his resigned agreement.

I recall that moment often in part because even as a child, I recognized how people in neighborhoods like ours felt talk was cheap, especially when it came from politicians. We were so used to being disappointed by the community itself that folks couldn't even imagine things being any different.

When I started working to change that, my mom's words were like an echo in my head, joined by a chorus of others who felt the same. I understood that when things looked bad, it was hard to inspire people to think about a beautiful future for themselves. As one of those who decided that our life's work was in community development, I figured it was our job to give people reasons to be hopeful by creating things they could see.

Much of the community work that I saw happening in my neighborhood was *advocacy-based* community development, which focused

71

on creating programs and policies to improve the quality of life for communities. I wanted to do *project-based* community development. I saw it as a complement to advocacy. It also seemed like a much more fun and fulfilling way to flex my creative muscles.

At the end of the day, week, or year, I wanted people to see and experience what had physically changed, and hopefully influenced the way we saw our community and ourselves within it.

A quote attributed to Jimi Hendrix sums it up nicely, "You have to give people something to dream on."[1]

CHAPTER 10

GARBAGE AND A GOLDEN BALL

My neighborhood is on a peninsula, with water on three sides. This made the area an attractive location for city- and state-sanctioned environmental burdens, as well as an inspiration for all the positive waterfront uses one can imagine.

The National Park Service had devised a plan to bring more public attention to parks by commissioning artists to highlight and interpret them.

The Swedish-born, Massachusetts-based public art design team of Mags Harries and Lajos Héder had the idea to float a seventy-five-pound gold-leaf-covered ball down the twenty-eight-mile length of the Bronx River as a way to metaphorically connect all the communities the river flowed through—from the wealthy communities in neighboring Westchester and Upstate New York to the poorest down in my neck of the woods.

I was a cofounder of a loosely formed network of community-based groups; city, state, and federal agencies; educators; and local businesses called the Bronx River Working Group (BRWG). All the participants were interested in the ecological, educational, economic, or some combination of restoration for the Bronx River, the only true freshwater river in all of New York City.

The BRWG was the brainchild of Jenny Hoffner, then the coordinator of Partnerships for Parks at the New York City Parks Department. She was responsible for creating partnerships between local communities and the parks that were in them—such as park conservatories or Friends of XYZ Park. Groups like that didn't generally exist in communities like ours.

Jenny did not have an easy job, especially with groups working in the lower reaches of the Bronx River. I was chief among the annoyances she had to deal with because I had more pressing issues on my mind.

The city and State of New York were planning to close the Fresh Kills Landfill on Staten Island, the site where almost all of New York City's household trash had been dumped for decades. Their plan was to redirect municipal waste to the same low-income communities of color, like mine, that were already home to nearly all of the city's commercial waste facilities.

Fresh Kills needed to close. In fact, it was used illegally by the city as a landfill for its entire history. It was supposed to have been a transfer station, designed to be sort of a repacking area for trash that was meant to be disposed of elsewhere. Because there was not enough political will to come up with a well-designed plan for waste reduction, recycling, and reuse, that site became a landfill by default.

As it drew near its maximum capacity, the city once again did not expend much meaningful energy on creating a sustainable solid waste management plan. Officials took what they thought was the path of least resistance, siting new facilities in politically vulnerable, low-income Latino and Black communities in the South Bronx, Southwest Brooklyn, and Southeast Queens.

In the South Bronx, it seemed as though the city was counting on the community not making much of a ruckus. The city had accepted the proposal of a newly formed company to handle 5,200 tons per day of New York City's waste at a facility to be built on my neighborhood's waterfront. The company even brought in a retired football player for what its leaders bafflingly considered "star power."

The project also had the backing of a grassroots group that claimed the community wanted this project. The group was promised a small percentage of the fees that the company would charge the city to handle the waste, and the grassroots group promised to use that money to promote further environmental advocacy in the South Bronx. Almost all of our elected officials didn't seem to notice anything wrong with the deal or openly welcomed the company.

Who was going to come to our defense? Who would say, let alone do, anything? Turns out, lots of people!

Back in the mid-1990s, before the social media era and even before the internet was widely used, there was a group of mothers and day-care providers that called themselves the Hunts Point Awareness Committee. They were the first to raise environmental quality issues in the area when they spoke out against the stench from the New York Organic Fertilizer Company, which processed sewage sludge into fertilizer nearby.

It took years of subsequent advocacy from several community groups, including my old organization, Sustainable South Bronx, which worked with the Interfaith Center for Corporate Responsibility to buy stock and initiate a shareholder action to get the company to first clean up its act and finally, leave.

A place that once processed stinky sewage sludge and degraded the local quality of life for tens of thousands of people is now a huge five thousand-person-capacity event space that has brought joy to thousands. One of my favorite memories was glimpsing an informal parade of very happy Tejano music lovers, most of the men in cowboy hats and the women in short black skintight dresses, walking from the subway on the way to a big concert held at the venue.

Many local groups in the South Bronx were members of the Organization for Waterfront Neighborhoods. OWN was a loose connection of community-based organizations from low-income communities of color from around the city. All of us were being discriminated against on environmental grounds because the city kept siting burdensome facilities in our midst. We were all working to promote a more sustainable waste management plan for New York City.

We were also members of the New York City Environmental Justice Alliance. At the time, it was powerfully led by my mentor, the late Leslie Lowe, a beautiful and fierce Black woman (partially raised in The Bronx too!). The organization supported local groups to defend public gardens when the city tried to bulldoze them and forced the city to acknowledge and work to repair the damage that its polluting policies caused communities of color.

José E. Serrano, the congressman for the South Bronx from 1990 to 2021, noted the environmental burdens his district bore and worked to address them, years before most of us knew anything about them.

All of this was really important work, but I get it. Most people don't think of trash, sewage sludge, recycling, or even public space as the most scintillating of topics. It ain't sexy, and in general, I don't disagree.

Regardless, people very passionate about all those things, present company included, knew that most people would need other reasons to see why they were important. I saw an opportunity for our community in what could be described as a frivolous golden ball afloat on our beleaguered river.

Helping People See beyond What's There

The organization that I worked for at the time hosted several community meetings. Although we never got hundreds of people to show up to the "re-envisioning sessions," as we called them, the steadfast neighbors who did come all talked about the kind of things they wanted to see in the neighborhood.

Better housing options. Good jobs. Nice places for people to work and play. Simple stuff that everybody wants. They said nothing about a sustainable solid waste management plan, although folks definitely wanted cleaner streets.

That's when I first met Jenny. In the spring of 1998, she kept coming around the community organization I worked for. She told me all about this small grant program that the US Forest Service was offering to groups that were interested in the restoration of threatened urban waterways, and the Bronx River was certainly one of them.

Once an ecological wonder that only rivers can be, snaking along twenty-eight miles of landscape through the elegant geometry of twists and turns, it maintained its own health as it provided habitats for countless animals and plants until Robert Moses, New York State's "master builder" and champion of cars, decided that he wanted to build a parkway. His plan was to straighten the river itself to provide an easier passage and nicer view for drivers.[1] Ironically, he named the parkway after the river he thoughtlessly mangled.

It was an engineering feat and an ecological tragedy.

By the 1990s, scrap metal yards and auto parts and repair shops lined much of the river's banks. Almost none of the river's industrial neighbors used the river for transport, although lots probably dumped into it.

The river went through actual parks farther north, but most of it was overgrown and it was hard for most Bronx residents to even see the river. The river also ran through the internationally acclaimed Bronx Zoo, but the Wildlife Conservation Society, which managed the zoo, erased The Bronx from the river, referring to it as the Yangtze River, where water buffalo and other water-loving animals were placed to roam.

Except for a few dedicated folks such as members of the original Bronx River Restoration,[2] which had been focusing on the river and what its restoration would mean for our borough and to the city since the 1970s, it was uncommon for people to consider the Bronx River a meaningful part of our landscape.

I didn't consider it at all.

On the New York City subway map, I could see the river abutting my neighborhood. However, it didn't register as a river to me, even though it was a nearly three-hundred-foot span of water under the bridge that separated Hunts Point from its neighbor, a community called Soundview. I would jog over that bridge to get to the only large green space nearby, Soundview Park.

So, here comes Jenny, calling me and visiting me every now and then. She was encouraging of my activism in general, and specifically, she urged me to apply for the seed grant program that her organization was offering to do restoration work on the Bronx River.

Jenny was awesome, so I liked her visits. She was from the South and introduced me to alternative Southern rock, which I didn't know was a thing. However, I dodged her attempts to get me to consider Bronx River advocacy in addition to the sustainable solid waste work that occupied much of my bandwidth.

That all changed when I went jogging early one morning with my dog, a rowdy eighty-pound shepherd mix named Xena. Yes, I named her after *Xena: Warrior Princess*—I loved that show! As I did most days on my run, I went down Lafayette Avenue and into the industrial section en route to Soundview Park.

This time, instead of turning left at Edgewater Road, Xena bolted straight, pulling me behind her. She had dragged me into the dumping ground that I had seen from the street for years but never ventured into it. Why would I do that? Yes, *why*, Xena!

I was afraid to let go of her leash and lose her to whatever was in there and equally nervous about what we would find together. But having a eighty-pound, slightly crazy but very protective dog made me settle into the adventure of it all.

I saw weeds and piles of garbage well over my head. There was a two-foot-high mound of chain with links as big as footballs. I wondered why on earth someone would go to such lengths to drag something so heavy here.

And there was the smell. Believe it or not, even with all the garbage, it didn't stink. It smelled fresh almost. I couldn't place what it was, and it seemed so out of context.

Xena sniffed along. I kept her close and we picked our way through.

Finally, I saw a light ahead of us through the weeds. We kept moving and there it was—the Bronx River.

Nearly three hundred feet of water lay before me, ending at a shore on the other side of the river. The banks were overgrown with what was probably some type of invasive species, but in my mind, it was a lush and verdant coastline.

Sunlight was glinting off the water, and it reminded me of golden birds lighting on the water just to delight me. And a gentle but crisp breeze gave me a whiff of success to come.

"This. This is the beginning of my neighborhood's transformation," I thought. I might have even said it out loud. *"This is how we are going to show that we are more than the trash that our city and state believe we are. Watch me."*

At some point, I had let Xena off leash to sniff around the "shore," which was just a broken retaining wall separating us from the tide that hadn't gone out yet. I hastily put her back on the leash, ran up the hill to my house, and wrote the proposal for the seed grant Jenny had been talking about. Xena didn't have much of a run that day, and I always give her credit with helping me discover that park.

That really was the start of my career. Thank you, Xena, RIP.

After that, I was deep into all things Bronx River, which was per Jenny's plan all along! She played the long game. She was smart enough to know that she should find folks who were active in neighborhoods *along* the river, not necessarily working *on* the river and sooner or later, we'd find a way to work the river into our own plans for our future. And boy, did I!

I loved being a part of the team that later became the Bronx River Working Group. We were a motley crew of organizations and agencies all banded together by our love of the river. At times we were openly at odds with each other outside our meetings. For example, my organization was in a legal battle with the agency of a fellow member, the New York State Department of Environmental Conservation, about the way it was siting waste facilities in our community. Still, we found ways to work together on the river.

Jenny would say, "Let's agree on what we can agree on." That's the attitude that I still take with me on my path as I work on all my projects. I have no problem with strange bedfellows. I don't believe people even have to like each other to do good work together. Unless you really are trying to date them, which I understand could complicate things.

Anyway, at one of our meetings, the subject of the National Park Service golden ball project came up. After copious peals of laughter and *way* too many bad jokes about a golden ball floating downriver amid debris and even the turds that escaped from the combined sewage outfalls after a heavy rain, we all saw that it could be a great opportunity to highlight all of our respective work along the river.

We'd turn that golden ball into the *Golden Ball*, a party that moved along the land as the ball floated along the twenty-eight miles of the river.

Those of us in the southernmost reaches of the Bronx River saw it as an awesome excuse to have a block party with DJs, performances, games, and canoe rides. The problem was that my little transformation experiment was still very much a dump when we decided on a date for the procession, several months later on Earth Day, April 22, 1999. We needed to get to work.

Working Out My Own Issues

Despite the joy of figuring out how the river was going to make our community dreams come true, it was a difficult time for me.

My dad's health was failing and Medicare did not cover much in the way of home healthcare. We had one wonderful home healthcare aide for a month or two, but after that, we were on our own.

My mom had lost tons of weight, seemingly overnight. She had been "pleasantly plump"—in other words, fat—for as long as I could remember. She was not taking care of herself as she took care of my dad, who was not getting better.

It was hard watching the dynamic between my mom and dad during his last months on earth. Sometimes she would lash out with bitter words even as she performed the most intimate tasks of caring for my father. My father would repay her in kind in his own lackadaisical drawl.

I could tell that they were both afraid and beyond stressed. They were not in a good place financially, and my dad's medical needs were difficult to manage. My self-appointed job was to be helpful so that both of them could have some peace. That meant that every day during the week, I was at their house for part of my morning before work, after work, and sometimes on breaks to help out with whatever was needed—weekends too.

My work on the river provided much-needed mental space for me to be creative and useful in a different type of way. Talking about my work to my parents seemed to take their minds off of their present conditions. They both even seemed to enjoy it, asking lots of questions, laughing about me being an environmentalist because of how much I would complain about dirt, heat, and worms whenever I attempted to help my father in his plot in the community garden outside our house. But mostly they were very encouraging and just plain curious.

My father died in January 1999, so he never got to see my work on the river in person. I reckon they both wished I had continued my childhood ambition to become a neurosurgeon and live in a fancy suburb.

Instead, I was squatting in a house across the street from them. I regularly worked a minimum of sixty hours a week at my job at the community center (which averaged out to about $10 per hour) doing something important that they knew I loved. I know that they were very proud of me.

The river remained my muse, always inspiring me to dream bigger for my community. It arrived in my life when I really needed something to focus on that was bigger than myself. The date of the Golden Ball was months away in April 1999, but working on that and other river-related projects kept me going and focused me on what I truly believed my purpose to be.

Playing My Part

Statistics showed that the asthma hospitalization rates in the South Bronx were seven times higher than the national average, due in large part to the diesel truck traffic that raged through our streets. And when a young girl named Crystal Vargas was killed by a truck while riding her bike on her block, which bordered a truck route, that tragedy added even more fuel to my desire to make our community safer and healthier.

As a response, I coauthored a study with Columbia University to determine the effects of pollution levels on community health,[3] which was to be used as a lever to advocate for truck traffic rerouting that prioritized pedestrian safety. My mother and I were a part of the team of community researchers tasked with collecting the data needed for the study: we sat on street corners in the predawn hours with air-testing equipment and counted trucks as they rumbled by.

I organized and performed in street theater projects such as the Hunts Point Trash Parade, where I, along with other intrepid souls, made costumes out of or resembling trash and handed out flyers about upcoming community meetings. One of my favorite times was when my friend, neighbor, and world-famous dancer and choreographer Arthur Aviles danced down Hunts Point Avenue in a burgundy full-body unitard with pieces of trash attached to it: cans, crumpled-up paper, and I believe even a dog toy that looked like a half-eaten chicken leg. I joined him, handing out flyers while sporting my own design of a fitted, one-shouldered peplum dress fashioned from blue plastic recycling bags. I completed the ensemble with dangling earrings made from Pepsi cans. All items were later recycled, of course.

A more sustainable solid waste management plan for our city that didn't openly discriminate against poor communities of color was needed. We also needed some joy and levity.

Okay, maybe I needed them, and I figured others could use some as well.

CHAPTER 11

DESPITE INCREDULITY, PLANNING WITH JOY

Fighting against big, awful injustices was necessary, but it was also spirit-depleting. It hurt my soul to always be fighting against something. I also wanted to build toward something I loved.

Our lives were hard enough. We were a poor community of color, the type of place that most people wanted to grow up and get out of. We needed something to feel good about, whether it was in the community or literally inside the house I grew up in, so that we could be hopeful about our future. I threw myself into Golden Ball planning.

Each of the groups working along the river started to plan individual events specific to a group's area, so we knew that we would be unable to attend each other's events. We still wanted the experience for anyone who went the entire way or even just part of the way to be memorable and recognize that we were all part of the same river project, so we tried to come up with a way to unify us. Someone suggested that Arthur could choreograph dancers to dance along the shore to accompany the ball on its journey and Charles Rice-Gonzalez, a local writer and publicist, could do our public relations. Check!

And then there was all the work to make it so that the ball could even float down the river and not get stuck—it had that much debris throughout it. My little street end wasn't the only area on the Bronx River that had been used as a dumping ground.

Old refrigerators, discarded clothing—if you could name it (and even if you couldn't), you could probably find at least one of those items slung into the shallow depths of the river. Jenny told me that volunteer groups found an odd contraption that they finally figured out was a penis enlargement apparatus—and one human skull. Not a fresh one, at least.

It was a heavy lift, literally, for volunteers, community groups, and agencies to get the river and the shore anywhere near presentable for our planned festivities. For example, community groups such as Youth Ministries for Peace and Justice mapped out where dozens of trashed cars were. Those cars were then hoisted from the river by the US Army Corps of Engineers—all we had to do was ask.

Beyond my little street end dump—or, as I referred to it aspirationally, my "park"—the river opened up into the Long Island Sound. My park was to be the last stop of the Golden Ball. And it really was the biggest dump.

Somehow or another, the story of this Black chick from one of America's most inner, inner-city ghettos, whose feisty dog pulled her into a dump that turned out to be an abandoned street end that dead-ended at the Bronx River, was interesting to the media. More times than I remember, I would proudly walk a reporter through the neighborhood, greeting folks I knew along the way. Once we arrived at the park, I would regale the reporter with how Robert Moses must be turning over in his grave knowing that we were building a new vision of hope and possibility on top of the failed remains of one of his last projects.

The reporter would look around at the detritus that invariably still covered the ground. The park was always in some stage of the long, slow process of a community-led cleanup effort operating with few resources—it always resembled a dump, despite our best endeavors. Then, without exception, the reporter would take a deep breath, and especially if it was low tide, I could tell that they didn't see or smell the future that I knew was right around the corner.

Not once was I ever bothered by that. They'd see it soon enough.

An Unorthodox Path for Community Change

At times, I felt as if I was very much alone among neighborhood organizations in terms of the vision to transform this street end into an asset the community would treasure.

Early on, I hosted a meeting with as many of the community-based organizations I knew in the area. Most did not send a representative to attend, so I had to have individual meetings.

None of them considered building a park a priority. Issues such as education, tenants' rights, health, and solid waste advocacy were at the top of their list. And although none of them came right out and said it, I sensed that they thought I was a bit of a dilettante in the social justice world.

It's true that I did not fit the mold:

- I didn't get involved in any type of advocacy until I was almost thirty, well beyond that youthfully exuberant stage in your life when you think you know everything.
- I went to my first protest after I turned thirty when I got involved in solid waste advocacy.
- I never said it out loud, but I often wondered who the cute guy with a beret was who often appeared on T-shirts favored by both politically correct white kids and progressive people of color before I figured out it was Che Guevara.

I had no idea that there was a lot of in-fighting between social justice organizations for resources, media attention, and staff, as well as bragging rights for the most socially conscious. And since I talked to anybody and everybody, I didn't realize that there were silos within and outside the community organizing world that one was not supposed to really get along with. You were to hold them at arm's length, in particular the business community, government, and rival community groups.

My ultimate goal was to show my colleagues and the world that if the community had a nice place for ourselves, that could inspire all of us to strategize and work more clearly toward a future we wanted to create for ourselves.

I was unaware of all the ill will I was generating among some of my peers. I took their lack of interest in the park's development as meaning that they wanted to see something before they believed that my plan could be an effective project for the neighborhood. I could respect that. My mother said the same thing, after all.

They didn't offer any assistance, endorsements, or opposition. They just left me to my work.

The first cleanups didn't attract a whole lot of community members. I had to ply people with free lunches and even that yielded scant results. I recognized that for most of my neighbors, a park on our waterfront was just way too far out of the realm of possibility. Even after a half dozen or so sparsely attended cleanups, the park still looked like a junkyard.

I had much more success with corporate groups wanting to "give back" to underprivileged communities like ours. The parks department would supply rakes, shovels, gloves, and garbage bags, and those groups would swoop in and clean up a bunch. I was grateful for the help, although I did wish more folks from the community would show up.

We were able to wrangle enough city, state, and business support to eventually make the site presentable.

ConEd, our local utility company, provided us with four heavy equipment operators and their vehicles. They were used to dig up old streets and utility lines, and they pretty much cleared the entire block of all the debris.

One of the ConEd crews consisted of all Christians who attended the same church. They looked at the project I was proposing as part of

God's plan to improve the neighborhood through me. They said they would put me and the park on their prayer list. I believe that they did.

The New York City Department of Transportation paved a meandering walkway as per our design all the way from the street to the river. The parks department poured wood chips in all the areas that our walkway did not cover.

Bette Midler brought all of her charm, her star power, and more than eighty skilled volunteers to do a big landscaping project through the group she founded, New York Restoration Project. At one point during all the action, I was talking with Bette, but she seemed distracted by something over my shoulder. Then she flashed that beautiful, twinkling smile of hers and said, "You look like somebody's *proud* mama!" I turned and saw Mommy, showing all of her pretty new Medicare-provided dentures, gazing at me with a smile that melted my heart. I was so happy that my mom finally saw what I'd been up to all that time. That was my favorite part, but other great things happened as well.

A local concrete plant dropped off concrete blocks that we used as seating, and we painted them with a gold auto body paint donated by a wonderfully eccentric guy who was a big supporter of graffiti art.

I also used some of the other donated paint to enliven the corrugated metal fence that separated the park from a scrap metal yard on one side and the world's second largest food distribution center on the other side, with pink, blue, and yellow polka dots of various sizes—inspired by Detroit artist Tyree Guyton. I would get up at the crack of dawn and walk down the hill to the park in my shabbiest work clothes, pushing a shopping cart filled with paint cans and brushes and a plastic tarp because I didn't want to get paint on the wood chips. Usually, I was alone walking down there, but occasionally I would happen upon a prostitute who would side-eye me. I would always offer a cheery "Good morning!"

I would stay in the park painting until I had to go to work and then pushed my cart up the hill, looking for all intents and purposes as if I had slept under a bridge. But I was so happy.

The Saturday of the Golden Ball was forecast to be a glorious day, so I made one last dash to paint more dots on the fence as the backdrop for the stage, which would host performances by the local senior citizen salsa dancing troupe, a DJ, Arthur's closing dance, and a myriad of speeches, including mine.

As I left the park, satisfied with my work and smiling from ear to ear, I encountered one of the most beautiful women I'd ever seen. Her skin was mahogany, her hair was cutely coiffed, and she had dressed her banging body in a tiny minidress. She was definitely a sex worker, but she hadn't been ravaged by the drugs that usually find their way into the lives of women like her.

"Hi!" she called out brightly as I walked past her. "Whatcha been doing in there? Oh! You're the one that's been painting those circles!"

"Yeah, that's me! I'm getting it ready for a festival we are having there today—you should come!"

No sooner were those words were out of my mouth than I saw an older and much more wasted looking prostitute approaching us with her pimp right behind. I didn't want any part of them, but I was afraid for this beautiful young woman too.

"Come today and I can get you help."

She smiled and looked over her shoulder.

"Oh, I'm okay. They aren't bad to me."

The other two kept their distance but stared me down as they walked past.

"C'mon," the pimp barked at the girl. "Let's go. Now."

"I'm coming. Have a nice time today!"

And she was on her way.

I watched them until they got into a car and drove off. There I was standing stupidly in grungy, paint-splattered work clothes and my shopping cart full of paint and I wondered if there was anything else I could have done. I offered up a prayer that she would find her way out of that life.

Then I trudged up the hill with my cart and went home, cleaned myself up, took a nap, and then went back down to the park for the festivities.

We Did That!

Well over one hundred people showed up! There was dancing! A live DJ and break-dancer named Crazy Rock! Games! Canoe rides! Free hot dogs!

The actual Golden Ball was rolled onto land from the river in a specially made gurney pushed by the artists and the procession led by Arthur and two other dancers wearing swirling gold lamé capes. And although I don't remember it all, I gave a speech about how we as a community can build beautiful things together.

I saw one of the women whom I had spoken to about the park project some months back. She was never particularly nice to me and today was no exception. However, she gifted me with a beautiful compliment, and I graciously received it, even though it was delivered through her clenched teeth: "You did a good job here. This is nice."

I claimed them all as part of this success, even if they didn't claim me. I motioned between the two of us and then gestured to the entirety of the Golden Ball revelers. "We did this!"

I saw the fruits of my labor being lovingly enjoyed just as I had intended. Community members happily enjoying a unique natural resource in their own community—who would have thought?

I knew that if it was built, they'd come. But there was just so much more to build.

CHAPTER 12

STAY IN YOUR LANE

My faith reminds me that there is nothing I can do to *earn* God's love. It is simply there, available to experience. However, there was this one glorious day—the kind I felt sure that God made special just for me.

I was in a great mood because one of my favorite projects, the one that we couldn't get any traction on for years, was showing great progress. I knew that it could impact my community in a beautiful way, and I'd been working my Holy Hustle so skillfully that God couldn't help but say, "Well done, baby girl. Enjoy your day!"

Yep. I woke up like that, as Queen Bey would advise anyone to say when we knew we slayed!

First, I spent time with God, meditating, reading scripture, and praying.

Then, I crushed my workout, thanks to a 0 percent financing deal for a Peloton bike delivered and set up in my basement days before. Walking downstairs for a spin class at the crack of dawn and then cooling down with a yoga class was at my fingertips, a very pleasurable, necessary, and strategic application of self-care.

And in the face of really bad health statistics among Black people, especially Black women, maintaining my own physical health is a message I can translate to everyone who sees me—we need and deserve to take care of ourselves. Taking care of ourselves can truly be an act of defiance, and I really encourage you to put yourself first sometime.

So after my usual spirit-filled, sweaty, defiance ritual, a lovely breakfast was prepared for me by my husband, James. He does pretty much all the cooking in our house. Our delicious breakfasts usually consist of egg whites and lots of vegetables. I am prediabetic and I struggle with high cholesterol and my weight, damn genetics. James lovingly accommodates all the dietary restrictions I place on myself, even though he can and does eat anything he wants, he rarely exercises, and his blood work still looks like that of a very healthy man half his age. Sometimes I hate him.

Our conversation over breakfast was charged with excitement for the day. We had acquired a historic former rail station in our neighborhood a few years back, and today I was going to be interviewed for a documentary about new real estate developers, produced by actor and real estate developer Malik Yoba.

Our building was designed by renowned American architect Cass Gilbert, also known for the iconic Woolworth Building in lower Manhattan, the US Supreme Court building, and other early twentieth-century gems. That station was a big part of why Hunts Point became my hometown.

My father was a Pullman Porter. Pullman Porters were a once vast network of Black men who traveled and worked along what was the most advanced system of transporting people, products, and information. It was no coincidence then that these men, having seen how differently people lived across the United States, Canada, and Mexico, were among those who formed the core of the early NAACP (National Association for the Advancement of Colored People).

My dad wanted to live out his American dream of homeownership, and since he often worked on the Harlem–New Haven–Hartford line, the idea of walking to and from work by way of the station in Hunts Point was very appealing to him. The Hunts Point Station had been closed to passenger service in the 1930s, but there was talk of reopening it into the late 1930s, right when my dad was looking to buy a home.

He had just won $15,000 by "playing the ponies," betting on a horse at a Los Angeles racetrack during one of his cross-country hauls. He came back east and made the single biggest investment in his life with the purchase of 651 Manida Street. Six of my ten older brothers and sisters and I were born or raised there.

The efforts to reopen the station to passenger service ultimately failed, and the station was subdivided and converted into storefronts. However, my father did use his train-workers club membership to get fellow brothers-in-rails to slow the train down enough as they passed the former station for him to jump off and scramble up the hill to the Jewish and Italian immigrant enclave that characterized mid-twentieth-century Hunts Point.

In the 1980s, a man named Jobo Salazar leased the station house and established the infamous topless bar called El Coche that occupied one of the storefronts. El Coche's sign proclaimed "Dancers Every Night," and the bar greeted passersby daily with a silhouette of a tired-looking woman and chasing multicolored lights beaming from the narrow window of the middle storefront for decades. Mr. Salazar died in 2011 with no clear direction about the future of either his business or the lease.

Amtrak, the building's owner, not wanting to be in the landlord business, evicted the remaining commercial tenants: a beauty salon, an insurance/travel agent, a fruit stand, and a pizza shop, among others.

The building stood at the gateway to the neighborhood, within a short walk to a major public transportation hub and our local shopping district. It was the primary way pedestrians came into and out of the neighborhood. Small businesses had occupied the building since the 1940s. But the last round of businesses moved on to new spaces, one by one as per the eviction orders. Now that it was abandoned, it sat there, getting tagged with graffiti, and not the cool kind.

The building had potential. My office was on the second floor of a building across the street from it. I often admired the row of pagoda-shaped dormers that defied the architectural vernacular of all the other buildings in the area. It seemed a shame that this unique little building would be left to sit there idly.

One morning, I was looking at the station through the window of my office. The idea of it sitting there like that put me on edge. It reminded me of growing up in the 1970s and seeing many vacant storefronts that would often become crack dens.

By nature, I like to build things or build them up when they need a little love. When I looked at that building, my revitalization spirit kicked into overdrive.

Our community deserved a gateway enlivened with activity, commerce, and beauty. The classic lines of the Cass Gilbert–designed Hunts Point Station offered the opportunity to achieve all three, given the right care, vision, and financial support. I knew my company had the care and vision part in spades. Getting financial support was something I knew I had to figure out.

Something needed to be done. I'm certain I was not the only one who felt that way, but as far as I could tell, no one else was attempting to do anything about it.

I contacted Amtrak to ask about acquiring the building. I had no plan for it at the time, and besides, it was rumored that Amtrak was notoriously hard to engage. I put a recurring entry in my calendar to reach out at least once a month until I found someone to deal with. I figured I had plenty of time to come up with a plan.

I sent a cold email out on a Tuesday. I got a response within hours, suggesting a call the following week to discuss our proposed plan. Wait, what? Well, better come up with a plan.

We seized the opportunity to flex: my team and I brainstormed about possible uses for this odd little building sitting at the doorstep of our community. We compiled a panoply of needs and desires expressed to us directly and indirectly over the years and proposed a cafe/restaurant, an exercise/fitness center, coworking space, and a youth-centered activity/safe space, such as a highly programmed "teen-only club." Later on, we thought it would be an awesome idea for the entire site to be a restaurant incubator, in other words, a food hall for local chefs, since a lot of culinary talent came from The Bronx, but most of them practiced their craft elsewhere or didn't have a brick-and-mortar restaurant.

Our ideas, presented with confidence, were enough to convince Amtrak officials that they would work with us on our acquisition of the building.

It took several years of negotiations, surveys, appraisals, and favors from RAF Architects, Higgins & Quasebarth Historic Preservation, and Sillman Engineers and a top-notch legal team at Norton Rose Fulbright LLP, but ultimately, we were able to acquire the building for $1 and a promise to bear all the costs to redevelop it ourselves.

Seemed like a good deal at the time. But a funky old building in a community quite low on the redevelopment spectrum is not a slam dunk. Its architectural attributes had been covered for decades under layers of dropped ceilings, badly executed subdivisions, and a dubious design aesthetic.

We didn't have the cash or the access to capital needed to redevelop it on our own, so we knew we needed to start a joint venture with a financing partner. We figured our building and their access to capital could create something awesome together.

One Saturday during spin class at Crank Studio on the Upper East Side, I sat next to a gentleman named Marty Weinstein, who had the most beautiful wavy white hair I had ever seen. I'd seen him there before; he was always nice and friendly to everyone.

We struck up a conversation before class started; I mentioned that I was a real estate developer, and he said he worked in financing development deals. He was intrigued by our project and we became great friends along the way.

Even someone with Marty's track record had a hard time convincing people that our little rail station project was worth anything. The only real interest we got was from either check-cashing operations or health clinics, and they were the last uses I wanted to see there. We already had too many of those in the South Bronx. I could not stomach the thought of adding more uses that profited from the entrenched poverty of the community.

For example, you find many check-cashing stores in low-status communities. They charge customers to use their own money, whether it's for cashing payroll checks, paying utility bills, or purchasing money orders. Profit is derived from the high rates of those that are unbanked as well as the relative lack of financial literacy in low-status communities.

Abundant health clinics in low-status communities make most of their money from the federal, city, and state funds provided to treat health conditions prevalent in these communities. Several bodies of research indicate that those very health conditions are due in large part to issues associated with systemic racism[1] and the disparities in health that coincide with it,[2] so the clinics had a very profitable although specious foundation for their business model.

Eventually, Marty did find us a joint venture partner, but he too fell off. We realized that our partner was deep in other deals that would prevent him from investing what was needed. Fortunately, we amicably went our separate ways.

Over the years, we must have shown the place to dozens of potential partners who we hoped would see the value in investing with us and the community at this pivotal point in our history. However, no one saw the architectural gem or the promise of its future. No one could see the value of people from the community, or people from outside the community, wanting to spend money for the type of uses we were proposing.

We had to fall back and do what we could and pivoted to transforming the building into an event hall for music, weddings, conferences, or other short-term uses. It would require less capital than a fully equipped food hall, and we were confident we could manage the less complex operations ourselves. Still, it was depressing to walk by the building and have its potential scream out of its cute little dormers, even though no one else seemed to believe it.

One day in August 2019, James had an epiphany: the building was, indeed, a hot mess. No one could see what we saw, so we needed to change what they saw.

Other than the interesting dormers on the outside of the building, which, truthfully, were overwhelmed by the mismatched roll-down gates, you couldn't tell that the exterior was once covered in a stately brushed stucco and terra-cotta tiles. Because the interior had been subdivided and renovated so many times, the expansiveness and height and care put into the original design was lost to most visitors. The smelly evidence of raccoon habitation didn't help.

When we stopped to think about it, we realized that it really did require quite a bit of imagination to see what we knew the building could be. So we set out to show others.

Early one August morning, James rented a twenty-cubic-yard dumpster, had it parked in front of the rail station, and invited me to demolish the interior of the old pizza shop. Yes, it was our version of a date night!

Equipped with sledgehammers, drills, crowbars, shovels, and a wheelbarrow with a flat tire, our fifty-two-year-old selves filled that entire dumpster—to the amusement of anyone walking by.

It was hilarious to chat with folks who would stop us midwheel-barrowing to the dumpster to talk about how they used to have pizza in there and how they were so happy that something, *anything*, was going to happen, and they were wondering what "they" were going to do with it. I would tell them about our plans, which they loved, and said that the building was mine, so the "they" was "me"! Invariably, an incredulous look washed across their faces and their eyes would widen.

It took a little getting used to the fact that a Black chick from the neighborhood owned this place and was doing something with it. A pause would follow, then a smile.

"You mean concerts could go on in here? Really?" "I could rent it for my daughter's quinceañera?" "Laser tag?" These are real responses.

At the end of the day, as my husband and I surveyed our work, tired and filthy (figure 7), we felt like we were walking on air because of the positive response we were getting from our neighbors. Over the next few days, we had a steady stream of volunteers from the

FIGURE 7: James and Majora demolishing the rail station interior

neighborhood pack up the rest of the debris to fill the next twenty-yard dumpster.

Don't You Tell Me What You Can Do!

A few days later, on that beautiful day I spoke of earlier, Bronx-born actor and real estate developer Malik Yoba came to Hunts Point. He was filming his documentary, called *I Build New York*, about how New Yorkers navigate the world of real estate development, and he was particularly interested in how Black and Brown folks do it. He came to hear my story.

Malik Yoba. Came. To. Hear. My. Story.

We had a great conversation. I felt validated.

I practically floated on the way back to my house after the interview, but something didn't feel right. Yes, the sky was a brilliant blue without a cloud in sight. There was a slight breeze and no humidity so I wasn't sweaty at all. I strode along in my chunky Sorel platforms. The pleats on my orange dress bloomed out behind me. I felt like I must have looked like a hip-hop version of the Winged Victory but still I couldn't shake the feeling that something, *some thing*, felt off.

I was around the corner from my house, on a street usually busy with people, but literally no one was around. None of the guys who worked in the auto glass garages across the street were there. No one was coming in or out of the apartment buildings I walked past. I was completely alone.

Then a person turned the corner and came into my view.

They had helped organize a protest against me the year before. They accused me of selling out my community, being a "community destroyer," and stealing from the community. (More on that in chapter 13.)

Anyway, there we were, just the two of us. Alone and together. On an empty street.

I took a deep breath and prayed, "I know you are here, God. Thank you."

I stayed on the same path I was on, my eyes straight ahead, not veering over to make extra room. They walked by me, staying close to the building and muttering something I couldn't make out.

"Stop and turn around, Majora."

I don't know if it was my pride or God talking, but turn I did. And words came out of me: "Hey! How about we talk? Human to human. I get the feeling that you and your friends have some misunderstanding about who I am and what I do. You can talk *to* me, instead of *about* me. I'm right here."

By that time, they had crossed into the street and were two car lengths away. They turned back around but didn't come much closer. I knew God had put a force field around me.

They started yelling about how they didn't *need* to talk *to* me because they *knew* all about all the things I had done to destroy and gentrify the community. I was a liar and a thief.

I had stopped reading the posts they wrote about me years before, but they didn't share anything I hadn't heard before.

When I asked what evidence they had of all my alleged transgressions, their response was to hurl a long and not particularly creative string of epithets at me that referenced my race, gender, intelligence, and morality and negated my humanity. Then they said, "And you bring your White developer friends here."

Dang. The idea that I am gentrifying the community that I was born and raised in by investing in it was so completely silly to me, I was able to dismiss that comment immediately.

However, can't I do anything on my own? I have to *bring* White developers here? What am I? Chopped liver? And as if White developers are clamoring to work with Black women developers. In what universe?

Now, as most know, Black Americans historically have had less access to capital, so I've always known that I would have to partner to get any deal over a certain size done and would be happy to partner with anyone who valued and respected my role in the deal, including White developers. However, all the other developments that I had completed by that point were done on my own. And although I had attempted to partner with White developers, thanks to my friend Marty Weinstein, only one came close to working on a deal with me, and that fizzled too.

But here was a person who couldn't even fathom that I could be a real estate developer. I could be a White developer's henchman but not the developer. That was the only thing that insulted me, but I kept my cool and calmly said: "I am not *bringing* White developers here. I. Am. A. Developer. And I want more of us to do that."

They continued to pace around the edges of the force field and screech about how horrible I was.

"I'm happy to share what I do and why I do what I do anytime you want to actually have a conversation about it. I'm sure I can learn something from y'all as well. But this isn't helpful."

Eventually they walked away, throwing up their middle fingers for emphasis just in case I didn't get their point earlier.

I watched until they put a good deal of distance between us because you never turn your back on that kind of energy, and then I walked home. And yes, I did take a look over my shoulder every now and then.

I, my work, and my approach were so far out of the realm of possibility that they couldn't or maybe just didn't want to see me.

How White Supremacy Has Led to Learned Helplessness

One of the most effective and insidious effects of White supremacy is that it leads not only actual White supremacists but some people of color and their "allies" to support the misguided notion that poverty is a *cultural attribute* of low-status communities.

The nonprofit industrial complex (NPIC) comprises social justice activists, community organizations, philanthropy, and governmental agencies that all unwittingly (to be generous) support an operational theory that poverty is a constant to be stabilized—with occasional Cinderella stories emerging. The first part of the Bible verse John 12:8, "You will always have the poor among you," may very well be the underlying chord that brings people dedicated to the institution of the NPIC to bear, but without regard to the context of spiritual restoration, generosity, and gratitude in which those words were written.

The nonprofit industrial complex entrenches rather than enriches those who fall into poverty through no fault of their own. In other words, low-status communities will always need help because, as a class, they will simply never move in the right direction—despite billions of dollars spent year after year—for decades.

Most low-status communities I have come in contact with, including my own, contain a wealth of nonprofit programs designed to help people *adapt* to poverty. Food pantries, homeless shelters, after-school programs and homework help, job training programs, rental assistance, and rental housing lotteries for people in the lower income bands are abundant.

Other programs facilitate the extraction of the brightest talent from low-status communities. Think of the college readiness programs designed for a relatively small portion of high academic achievers among all the students with potential in low-status community schools. The assumption is that the talent from our communities is expected to migrate out, aka brain drain or bright flight. Put another way, that migration is the cause of a talent-retention deficit in low-status communities.

In contrast, far fewer programs are designed to move people out of poverty or generate wealth as they stay within their own community, such as homeownership support, financial literacy, credit repair, and business development workshops for aspiring entrepreneurs.

It is almost as if poverty is equated with neighborhood preservation, and thus those who most resemble the archetype of a poor person needing help are considered more authentic and representative of the low-status community. The lion's share of the nonprofit industrial complex's goodwill will be directed there to the neglect of a smaller number of people who are capable of succeeding, despite all the well-documented obstacles they face.

The problem with this kind of decades-old status quo community development is that the same type of poverty-level economic maintenance is continuously repeated. Poverty-level economic maintenance in low-status communities looks like this:

- Instead of banks and credit unions that could help people grow their money, check-cashing stores and pawn shops proliferate. All of these are regulated industries, but the geographic distribution is not regulated despite these businesses' impact on community development and talent retention.
- Instead of a diverse array of ways to feed yourself, like supermarkets, cafes, restaurants, and farmers markets, you'll find predominantly fast food and other unhealthy options. This

rather thin hospitality-sector representation belies more than just poor physiological nutrition. The lack of quality "third spaces" reduces community members ability to socialize, network, and grow as individuals or professionally. (More on this very important aspect in chapter 13.)

+ Instead of ways that encourage maintaining a healthy lifestyle through diet and exercise, you'll find more pharmacies and health clinics running lots of dollars through the community to treat lifestyle conditions prevalent in low-status communities, such as diabetes and obesity. You'll also find many options to self-medicate via ubiquitous liquor stores.

+ Instead of a vibrant mix of retail options, slight variations of dollar and discount stores will likely be your only options.

+ Instead of different levels of housing affordability for both renting and homeownership, you will find a high concentration of very low-income government-subsidized rental housing. These generate huge fees for a small cast of players in the multifamily real estate development industry while entrenching a landless class with little hope of breaking out and experiencing one of the most vaunted aspects of the American Dream—homeownership.

These projects create healthy revenue for some—almost exclusively outside the community. However, the net result is concentrated poverty and all the issues associated with poverty from poor educational attainment, decreased health outcomes, and higher rates of people involved in the justice system. I would also argue that concentrated poverty cements the perception of people from both inside and outside these communities that everything and everybody in them are simply of less value than others.

Yet despite the shamelessly repeated results of the poverty-level economic maintenance tradition in low-status communities, remarkably little has changed in the proliferation of these very types of "community development" that exacerbate the predictable outcomes.

For example, billions of philanthropic dollars have been poured into the South Bronx. However, poverty, unemployment, health, and education statistics continue to earn us the dubious distinction of being among the country's poorest congressional districts for more than thirty years straight. Why is community development in low-status communities so narrowly defined?

I don't presume much, but I have launched and continue to refine my concept for a much more holistic approach to low-status community development that starts from inside the community itself. I've learned that some see my approach as too far outside the realm of possibility for someone like me. Way too far for some folks.

CHAPTER 13

SELLOUT

"Haters gonna hate." A cousin of "All press is good press" and "Haters make you famous," this phrase has its roots in hip-hop but is now part of the American vernacular. It is shorthand for one's predilection and ability to dismiss the attacks of those opposed to one's success.

No matter what, if you are leading in your career, family, community, classroom, corporation, whatever, someone is going to notice you, and they will not like it. No matter what.

I got haters, but I don't like the word "hate" applied to people, myself included, so I decided to call them the Majora Carter Fan Club, or simply the "fan club," because they seem to spend so much time thinking and talking about me. I think some of them might have a little bit of a crush on me. So I guess it's kind of sweet?

But seriously, I have garnered some rants, criticism, and condemnations over the last couple of decades. It confirms to me that I am disrupting the status quo. I try to make sure that the energy we unleash through such disruptions is channeled toward the maximum benefit to others.

On nearly all occasions, when fan club members blurt out their acrimony regarding some part of my work, I reach out to them directly, but I am usually met with silence or further (usually social media) rumblings. The fan club members love talking *about* me but never can step up to the plate and talk *to* me.

Since I have never been able to engage in a real discussion with them, I can only offer my hypothesis: A more or less universal fear of change (no matter how bad things are now) coupled with the insidious effects of White supremacy work hand in hand to foment hatred of people of color *among* people of color. Please read that again. Historically, low-status communities' weakened position in American society remains entrenched by this sad cycle.

Think of J. Edgar Hoover and how he used his powers at the FBI illegally to draft Black folks to infiltrate the Black Panther Party. I don't pretend that this is as dramatic or historically significant as that, but you get my point.

Developing for-profit real estate to create projects designed to stop the hemorrhaging of talent from low-status communities is still a new take on how to address generationally entrenched problems.

For some, it must have seemed like sorcery.

When a Coffee Shop Is More Than Just a Coffee Shop

When folks from the hood express a desire to leave their community, there is often an assumption that they are leaving because of violence or crime. However, in countless discussions I've had with my neighbors, the desire to leave was fueled by aspirations for a lifestyle they did not see possible in their hometown. Seemingly mundane things like cafes, bars, and restaurants were often mentioned with a longing in their voice.

Opening a coffee shop seemed to me like a way to make at least some community members want to give our neighborhood a second chance before they bolted. While many community members understood and supported our goal for opening a coffee shop, a vocal minority not only didn't see but could barely acknowledge my humanity in the process.

"She's not human!" These hissed words from one of several screaming women, some of whom I had been acquainted with for years, were relayed to me by my friend and colleague José Galvez.

Those and a variety of other choice words were spat through tears or chants by a dozen or so protesters, mostly Latina women. I viewed the entire exercise as a dubious honor for me.

They had set up camp in front of the new location of our coffee shop, only two doors down from our old one. Brandishing hand-painted signs and bullhorns, they declared me a sellout, a gentrifier, evildoer, and a traitor of the community, among other monikers, creative and profane.

They were protesting me personally, as well as the coffee shop I had opened two years prior, which is an extension of my community-built-environment work over decades. They asserted that both I and that darned cafe were harbingers of gentrification in *their* community of the South Bronx, the neighborhood where I was born, was raised, and continue to live.

By their account, I was *the* cause of gentrification. They wanted to show the rest of the community (and me) how strongly they felt about it with a good old-fashioned public display of opposition (figures 8 and 9).

I learned about the protest because my friend Linda Gross, who works in media, was sent the press advisory, which she forwarded to me. She wrote the organizers and asked them to substantiate their claims against me and was met with a two-page response, littered with obscenities. It was actually pretty entertaining to see the alacrity with which they reported my evil omnipotence. It was barely a step below QAnon theories.

I can't say I wasn't expecting it. In fact, I was wondering why it took so long. There had been signs of contempt soon after I started working in the social justice industrial complex in the late 1990s. Maybe I should pause here.

"Contempt?" "Protests?" "The problem with opening a coffee shop in your own neighborhood is . . . ?" I get those and similar questions every time I try to explain my life to most people.

It seemed to me that in the social justice world, activists were very open to acknowledging the years of disinvestment that happened in our community. It also appeared to me that some of them simply

FIGURE 8: My protesters (*smiley faces added*)

FIGURE 9: Flyer distributed at protest

could not fathom the possibility that we could set up the conditions to have a high quality built environment, led from within.

Hipsters Aren't the Only Ones Who Drink the Blackest Beverage on the Planet

Although it is easy to imagine the motives for getting out of the hood include the threat of violence, crime, gangs, and abuse, young aspiring people who want to leave for greener pastures say they are not fleeing a horrible situation but seeking opportunity, equality, and a different lifestyle.

To that end, opening a coffee shop was a direct response to the results from our own market surveys. We documented how residents would leave the neighborhood for cool spots like restaurants, bars, and yes, coffee shops. We figured that if we built something cool, they might be open to buying those higher quality experiences in a nice place without leaving the neighborhood.

However, it was never lost on me that a coffee shop opening in an American low status neighborhood is considered synonymous with gentrification. It symbolizes that a neighborhood is changing but not for the benefit of residents already there.

Our coffee shop was part of our approach to real estate development, which creates lifestyle incentives that stem the tide of brain drain in low-status communities by giving people born and raised there reasons to want to stay and reinvest themselves emotionally, financially, and spiritually.

I reject the notion that specialty coffee shops *belong* to white hipsters with skinny jeans and ironic beards in gentrifying neighborhoods. Coffee came first from Africa, spread to the Middle East and Asia, and was brought via colonialism to the Americas. It is an intrinsic part of culinary cultures all over the world.

And coffee is the Blackest beverage on earth, thank you very much. Reclaiming a little piece of the specialty coffee market as a Black-owned business was apropos for our real estate and economic development.

Around the same time we were conducting our surveys, we learned that more kids from the South Bronx were graduating and going on to college than our community had seen in the past thirty years. As a community known mostly for all the things we lacked, it was nice to have a statistic to be proud of, some good news.

When my team surveyed some of those students regarding what they thought the community needed, they generally supported a typical litany:

- More low-income affordable housing
- More health clinics
- More homeless shelters
- More community centers
- More programs for the "kids," (which we thought was ironic since they were not much older than the kids they thought needed more community centers, even though they themselves were too cool to be caught dead in them)

Then they were asked, "If you do go to college and have a good career, are you going to come back here to live?" They would literally recoil.

What they believed their community needed more of were attributes that they considered markers of poverty. They were not aspiring to such things.

"Why would I do that? I want to live in a place that's nice. That has restaurants, nice shops, nice places to live in, things like that! There's nothing here!"

They complained about people not picking up after their dogs. There were more liquor stores than nice shops. Litter. They felt they lacked opportunities to connect with other aspiring individuals like themselves.

The survey results regarding things they wanted in the community of their dreams included the kinds of things not readily available currently. They wanted to be inspired by their community and the people in it.

They didn't believe that there could be great places to live, work, and play in their own neighborhood—it was just not possible.

Urbanists and others call these spots "third spaces" because they are neither work nor home but a little of both plus something extra. That extra is what the business does to create an environment that attracts people who add their own creative spin on it. But the crux of the challenge is that so many (my own family included) are steeped in a tradition of viewing where we live (and to a certain extent ourselves) as worthless.

They also wanted people around them who did interesting things in their lives, those from different educational backgrounds and incomes, making decent money in careers they loved.

Why couldn't our community have the kind of development that was responsive to their aspirations? We simply wanted to show that they didn't have to move out of their neighborhood to live in a better one.

Ready? Fire! Aim! Now I'm a Real Estate Developer!

Calling myself a developer was a bold claim from a chick with zero background in real estate development, but I had no formal background in anything I'd accomplished in my career, so why not? This was no different, although it was a lot more expensive. I didn't know when I started about OPM, other people's money. More on that later.

We developed a strategy that would facilitate the type of local economic developments that could create some jobs and positive social activity. We decided to focus on two major growth sectors in the economy: tech and specialty coffee.

We obtained two commercial leases with favorable terms in a building owned by SEBCO, the housing organization that redeveloped thousands of housing units in the South Bronx.

In one of the storefronts, we started our own tech social enterprise. The "social" part sought to create more diversity in technology. The "enterprise" part focused on providing some of the software services that New York City tech companies needed but could not get satisfactorily from offshore sources.

We were able to hire locally, giving young folks their first entry-level job in the tech sector and even setting some of them up for better paying jobs in the industry.[1] We won awards for innovation, but as happens to many Black tech founders, the appetite to invest in my enterprise to get it to scale was just not there. We dissolved the company within a few years.

The other storefront was reserved for a cafe. We looked far and wide for someone to operate a cafe there, hoping to pass on our favorable lease cost to them. We discovered a few passionate individuals who wanted to start a cafe but they had little capacity to do so, and those who knew the business had no interest in coming. For example, my email inquiry to Starbucks was met with silence, and when I randomly met a Starbucks real estate executive, he told me Starbucks considered our market far too "emerging" to warrant one of its stores there.

I found it ironic that after our cafe had been operating for more than a year, I ran into that same executive, who told me that Starbucks was looking at the area for a possible location. My heart sank when I heard that.

By establishing the specialty coffee market where there had been none, we had inadvertently helped the folks at Starbucks "discover" there was a market in my neighborhood, and they would take advantage of that. I knew their presence would likely have a negative impact on our little locally owned cafe based on the inferiority complex that systemic racism has placed on communities of color: communities tend to value major brands over anything produced by companies or individuals from other communities of color.

After a year of using the proposed cafe location as storage because nobody could or would open a cafe there, we decided to start up one ourselves.

Constructing a Third Space: A Joint Venture

We didn't know anything about opening up a cafe, but you wouldn't have known that from watching us!

We hired Doel Rivera's company as the contractor to build a space that we figured would work—it had exposed brick walls and lots of reclaimed wood leftover from one of his other projects. *Boom!*

To make the coffee, we planned on using the commercial version of the Swiss-based Nespresso system. *Check!*

It looked like any other cute little coffee shop in any urban area in the country. *We ready!*

Fortunately, before we opened in that configuration, one of the folks on our advisory board, Sulma Arzu-Brown, asked some friends who actually owned coffee shops to give us some advice. Those friends happened to be Jeremy Lyman and Paul Schlader, owners of one of New York City's premier coffee roasters with an attendant line of shops called Birch Coffee.

To our surprise, they were interested in partnering with us on a coffee shop in the South Bronx as a joint venture between our companies. We were excited when Sulma's family wanted to invest in the coffee shop as well, which was awesome because local folks investing in locally owned businesses is a part of our overall real estate development strategy that promotes generational wealth creation and retention.

It would be the first coffee shop we'd had in my neighborhood since I was in high school in the early 1980s.

I remember when Moshman's Delicatessen closed. It was one of the last remnants of old-timey Hunts Point, when mostly white folks lived in the neighborhood. I still miss the bagels.

James and I got a crash course in the coffee shop business—from roasting all the way to shop operations. We learned everything from customer service, inventory management, shop maintenance, staff training, and yes, even how to properly steam milk and pull espresso shots. My latte art game is rudimentary, but I can make an endearingly lopsided heart on a cappuccino.

Having experts on board was a godsend: we really learned how much we didn't know. We had to redesign the shop to make it code compliant and better functioning.

James or I or both of us were physically in the shop every day—
mostly James because I still traveled for speaking engagements and
consulting gigs, which paid our living expenses as well as some startup
expenses for the cafe. James was the barista on duty every single morning for the first several months.

Birch covered all inventory and equipment costs as well as payroll (although neither James nor I took a salary; our work was sweat
equity we put toward the operation). We covered rent, utilities, and
overall management and maintenance of the cafe.

It didn't take the Birch guys (or us) too long to realize that our partnership wasn't going to work out. Birch Coffee had established its very
successful niche by serving only excellent coffees, teas, chais, mochas,
and milks, expertly prepared by skilled baristas—no crazy flavors or
themed drinks. Just the idea of a Frappuccino was anathema to them.

The taste and craftsmanship of their work was exceptional, but
the local market was not accustomed to what they offered.

Bodegas on every other corner all sold $1 cups of drip coffee.
They were not our competition. Our competition was syrupy sweet
flavors, whipped cream, and other non-coffee-purist stuff that the
four nearby Dunkin' Donut locations had to offer.

They were mopping the floor with us. Watching people walk by
our windows with Dunkin' Donuts cups was heartbreaking. Our price
points were the same and our quality was better, but you couldn't get a
pumpkin spice latte at our shop.

Past the ring of Dunkin' shops that surrounded us, the closest
Starbucks was six subway stops away in either direction. Many folks
would leave our neighborhood (or pay for Uber Eats delivery) to par-
take in the status symbol of the North Star of "fancy" coffee. We know
because we saw plenty of Starbucks cups in trash cans and on the
street.

The writing was on the wall. If we were going to survive, we
needed to give the people what they wanted.

We had a very amicable decoupling after six months operating
as Birch Coffee. Paul and Jeremy left us all the equipment they had

purchased and a wealth of knowledge that we used to start fresh. We are forever grateful to them as the godparents of our new endeavor, this time 100 percent locally owned.

Second Time Around: Leaning into Community Culture

So there we were, owners of a locally owned cafe in the South Bronx. We decided to go full tilt back to the roots of one of the things that embodied the culture of the South Bronx, hip-hop itself.

First things first. The place needed a new name: the Boogie Down Grind Cafe was our choice. It embodied everything we wanted to convey. "Boogie Down" is the informal name of the New York City borough of The Bronx, mostly and affectionately applied to and by those of us residing in the South Bronx.

A little history for those of you who don't know. Back in August 1973, siblings Clive and Cindy Campbell hosted a party in the recreation room of their building, 1520 Sedgwick Avenue (figure 10). It was there that Clive, aka DJ Kool Herc, debuted his skills using two turntables and a mixer to isolate the grooviest part of a record. It is generally known and accepted that that party represented the birth of the worldwide phenomenon that is now called hip-hop.

"Grind" referred to coffee itself as well as what folks working hard to live out their best life do on a daily basis.

"Cafe" just sounded cuter than "coffee shop," and we knew we'd want to sell light bites as well as wine and beer too. At the time, the only places in the neighborhood to get a drink were the topless bars, which attracted only a certain type of crowd.

Our logo was designed by world-renowned graffiti artists TATS Cru (figure 11).

Our baristas, well-versed in the varied world of hip-hop music, all doubled as DJs and were in charge of the music played at the cafe. Our only rule was that it had to be family friendly, so they couldn't play the explicit version of songs. We hosted events celebrating the

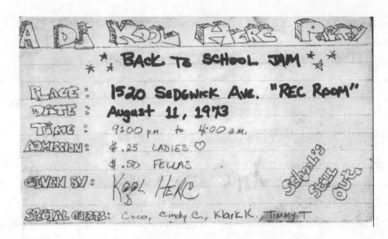

FIGURE 10: Flyer for an early DJ Kool Herc Party, 1973

FIGURE 11: Boogie Down Grind Cafe

work of local artists, authors, and entrepreneurs. And yes, we added syrup flavors and whipped cream to our menu and attracted a lot more customers.

However, we still operated at a loss. We knew it was going to be a matter of time before we showed any profits, but we were confident that we were cementing our presence in the neighborhood as a home-grown asset.

Fan Club Art Projects

Our little cafe was a source of great pride for James and me. Indeed, I met more people in the neighborhood from running the cafe than I ever did in all my years of activism. More importantly, the cafe allowed others in the neighborhood to meet each other.

Anyone who visited our cafe would question the perception that only the most vulnerable and dejected lived in our community. The folks gathered at the cafe for their daily brew, events, or even just a safe space to charge their phone and chat with someone interesting. They were seeking good things for their lives and it showed.

At our cafe, it was not uncommon to meet neighborhood residents who had degrees from Harvard and other storied institutions, owned their own businesses, or made incredible art. At the Boogie Down Grind, one could discover that aspirational role models lived nearby, and quite possibly, you would often find yourself being an aspirational role model to someone else.

However, between traveling for work, working on our other projects, and managing a cafe, other things in my life suffered. In particular, I was feeling like I was completely slacking in my exercise routine.

I was a big fan of spinning and I found a studio on the Upper East Side of Manhattan that I could afford. Crank Studio was owned by the son of a first-generation Puerto Rican family who once owned an auto glass shop in Hunts Point coincidentally. I was excited to support a business owned by a fellow Bronxite, but I didn't go to a single class in the months leading up to and the first month after opening our shop.

James knew I was missing it and encouraged me to take a Saturday morning off so I could attend a spin class.

I left the house early that Saturday morning—in time enough to hop on the subway to make it to a 7:30 a.m. class. On my way to the subway, I caught sight of one of the classic yellow smiley faces I had painted one day on a rusty gate that led down to the railway.

I've been obsessed with smiley faces since I was four years old, long before they became known as emoticons. I've collected them and have been known to paint them around the neighborhood to help make people smile.

From a distance, it looked like someone had added a nose to one of my yellow guys. I didn't mind when people would improve upon my work. It was just a smiley face for crying out loud. For example, a while back someone had added eyelashes to this one and I loved it. When it needed some freshening up after being in the weather 24-7, I even touched up their additions. And this one needed a touch-up anyway. I was eager to see what someone did with it. I got closer and realized it wasn't a nose. It was a sticker (figure 12). They had taken a quote that I used in a recent *New York Times* article to highlight what they really thought of me (figure 13).

In the article, I had used the term "self-gentrification," which I borrowed from Dr. Ronald Carter, former president of Johnson C. Smith University, an HBCU (Historically Black college or university) in Charlotte, North Carolina. During a conversation I had with him in 2012, he used the phrase "self-gentrification" to describe how the plan to ensure that the development the university was doing would benefit both the low-income community nearby and the campus itself.

I thought the use of the word "self" as a prefix to "gentrification" was indeed provocative. But it also suggested that people in those changing neighborhoods *wanted* to see improvement in their communities, that they weren't happy with the way their neighborhood was either—a sentiment that was reinforced by our survey data.

FIGURE 12: Defaced mural

The stickers were anonymously produced, although I have some idea about the creators. It was a good design too, which I kind of appreciated.

I snapped a picture of it on my phone, sent it to James, peeled it off, and proceeded to my spin class.

By the time I got back home, I heard reports from friends in the area that they had seen and removed about a half dozen of the same

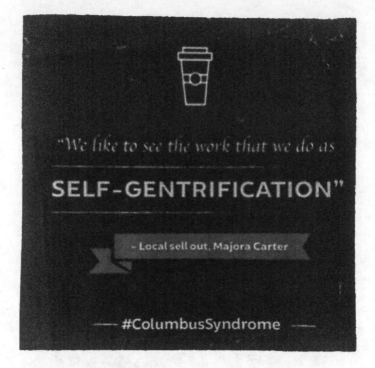

FIGURE 13: Defaced mural detail

stickers posted around the neighborhood. I took the sticker I had retrieved, mounted it and framed it nicely, and hung it in my office next to a wall full of actual awards. This was a trophy of a different sort.

Another sticker campaign followed. A mural of me painted as part of an art project that celebrated local leaders was defaced with stickers crudely emblazoned with "Trojan Horse Business." Neither campaign was very extensive, but their organizers, the Majora Carter Fan Club, gave it their all.

CHAPTER 14

CONTROVERSY
Teachable Moments

We decided to embrace the controversy and follow the example of the Queen herself: BEYONCÉ.

Beyoncé performed, or shall I say slayed, at the 2016 Super Bowl halftime show. She dominated the field in a sexy getup that evoked both the military and Michael Jackson. She was flanked by a multitude of beautiful Black female backup dancers donning Black Panther-esque berets and Afros with choreography wielded like graceful sledgehammers.

The day before the Super Bowl, she released a video of her song "Formation," a celebration of Black culture and an artful but blistering critique of police brutality.

One scene in the video featured a young Black boy in a hoodie dancing in front of a line of policemen in riot gear as the camera pans to a wall spray-painted with the words "Stop shooting us." It was an obvious reference to the murder of Trayvon Martin, a seventeen-year-old Black youth murdered by a self-proclaimed neighborhood vigilante who was later acquitted of second-degree murder.

Apparently, a Black woman celebrating her own talent, creativity, and culture while calling out the injustice of police brutality was too much for some pundits and law enforcement officials. They considered it too closely aligned with the Black Lives Matter movement and its alleged anti-police activism.

There were calls by some law enforcement organizations to boycott Beyoncé by not working at her concerts. I was unable to find any data about whether police officers decided not to sign up to work on her security detail, so who knows?

Beyoncé responded in a rare interview, declaring that some clearly misunderstood her message as anti-police and proclaiming her respect for officers that work hard to keep us safe. She straight up said those offended by her celebrating her culture or highlighting injustice had their own problems.

She also made a move that showed how comfortable she was in her own power and in business. She emblazoned "BOYCOTT BEYONCÉ" on T-shirts and sold them at her concerts. I bought one and it is one of my prized possessions. So a few months later, of course, I channeled Beyoncé!

Some folks upon hearing the term "self-gentrification" immediately gravitated to the "self" part because they wanted better things in their own community that served *them*. Others understood the concept but felt that the word "gentrification" was far too loaded to provide a foundation for a fruitful discussion.

At the time, I thought it was a way to bring people's attention to how community development expectations were based on whom the community was being developed for but as time progressed, it became clear that it was just too much of a trigger and stopped conversations before they even started.

And then there was the Majora Carter Fan Club, creators of the sticker campaign. I believed that even if I had used the term "Sunshine and Lollipops," they still would have hated it, in part because many of them are what are referred to in the policy world as Citizens against Virtually Everything, or CAVE People. Change is resisted, even when things suck. But when a woman of color is the one doing the change, people—many different kinds—have a hard time accepting it. Just ask Beyoncé. Or Serena Williams. Or Sonia Sotomayor. Or Amy Tan. Or Malala Yousafzai. Or Deb Haaland. Or me.

Regardless, I saw this as an opportunity for others within the community to share what they thought were great approaches to how we could create economic recovery from within the community itself.

We decided to host a gathering called the Self-Gentrification Salon. We used the sticker as part of the promotion.

The plan was to give folks, including my detractors, an opportunity to share what they thought was up. I wanted the community to have a chance to learn about developments that were happening in the community *by people from their own community*.

My invitations to those within the social justice community were met with silence and suspicion. They didn't come. I wasn't surprised.

The people who presented at the event were working on projects within their own communities:

- Nöelle Santos, a bibliophile and HR professional who decided to open up her own bookstore after the last bookstore in The Bronx closed down. Nöelle was also a wine connoisseur, so she combined her two great loves and planned to open the Lit Bar ("lit" as in literature as well as tipsy). Her shop was wildly successful from day one.
- Sulma Arzu-Brown, a proud Garifuna whose family emigrated from Honduras to Hunts Point when she was a child. A children's book author and communications professional with a family of her own, she bought the house she grew up in and was determined to be a part of the change in her own community. Her family was the first to invest in our cafe.
- Judith Raphael, aka Sukari, singer, actress, and professional clown whose creative hustle is legendary.
- Idelsa Mendez, a college educator and local homeowner who, after a scare with a potentially fatal health condition, had an intense appreciation for each new day that her life continued. One of the ways she showed it was by highlighting great things in her own community.
- Karen Haycock and Christopher Illum from Habitat for Humanity New York City also joined the panel. They spoke

of their agency's plans to build more opportunities for low-income families to own their homes in the South Bronx.

I really did want my fan club to attend. However, this was not the first time, nor would it be the last time, that they would choose to talk about me rather than to me.

But for the more than forty people who attended the event, the overwhelming response was excitement that folks in their neighborhoods weren't just complaining but actually *doing* something to make the neighborhood better in a structural sense that could allow others to build on that momentum and attract more capital. Some of them even bought the T-shirts we had on sale, printed with the sticker's graphic. I was unable to give the creators design credit or a cut of the proceeds because no one ever stepped forward to claim ownership of the design. Surprise.

Being Comfortable as a Target

Learning to be comfortable with being uncomfortable is something I decided to embody after several outsized and hostile responses to my efforts.

Back in 2013, I was a consultant for FreshDirect, an online grocery service that was planning to move to the South Bronx. That led to a yearlong social media campaign against me by a local activist group that culminated with me as the subject of a front-page (and *all* of page 3) *New York Times* article with the headline "Hero of the Bronx Is Now Accused of Betraying It." The group objected to FreshDirect primarily over environmental concerns and in part because they felt there should be more local community control over food production, such as urban farming.

I did not disagree on some of the group's objections. The city had done a grave disservice to the community by approving the company's move to an area that already had a great deal of truck traffic without conducting an environmental impact assessment and not informing the community about the city-subsidized deal until well after the ink was dry. That was really unfortunate because it was a decent company with a useful service for many applications and a progressive history of using alternative fuels for its vehicles.

FreshDirect's new location was zoned industrial, meaning any number of industrial uses could have been approved there. I shuddered to think of which of the typical, noxious facilities could have been sited there with very little recourse: oil storage tanks and delivery, a cement plant, a scrap metal yard, or a waste facility, among others.

A public-facing company such as FreshDirect would have a vested interest in being seen as a good neighbor. I was of the opinion that because it was a public-facing company, it could have been pushed to engage with the community on more impressive environmental progress and other issues that could impact the community positively.

But before I was even aware that there was a company called FreshDirect, some members of the activist group were contacting my office. Some exchanges bordered on harrassment—one person called and told our office manager, "Majora *better* fall on the side of the community!" Another person came to our office while my office manager was there alone. She met him at the door and when he demanded to be let in to see me, she explained that I wasn't there. She could tell that he didn't believe her. And yet another contacted us via email, attaching hundreds of pages of documents they wanted us to review before helping them fight FreshDirect. We asked if they could pay our initial consultation fee of $500 to cover our time and also suggested that we talk to see what else they were thinking about how we could be helpful. No response from them.

The *New York Times* article portrayed me as refusing to meet with the visitor because I didn't want to deal with the community. I was actually on vacation in the South of France after I had presented to a conference for urban planning professionals in Paris.

The article implied that my fan club accused me of profiting from the struggles of community members that deserved my support. One tweet from the fan club labeled me a "shadowy poverty pimptress." I was expecting them to call me a corporate whore, and who wants to be referred to as a whore? At least with "pimptress," they saw me in a power position, so I guess that's progress. I was equally amused by the writer's creative use of words. We may not agree, but I will always appreciate a good effort.

The *New York Times* put all its journalistic heft on what amounted to a gossip piece. Former clients of mine going back several years reported that they had been contacted by the reporter with questions that were clearly looking for dirt on me, as if to prove that I've always been the duplicitous snake that this group alleged. The piece referenced my looks more than the substance of the issue, even mentioning my "high-wattage smile." It is beautiful, and no cavities. At least that piece of the article could be considered objective journalism!

Ultimately, by accepting FreshDirect as a client, I knew I was putting a great big bullseye on my head and another on my back. With the focus on me, I figured the local organizations on the ground would be able to do their work with this company unencumbered, and there were some notable successes.

Those opposed to the company did not show any willingness to engage in dialogue, and they effectively silenced other activists who might have engaged constructively. I was approached by quite a few of them who told me, furtively, making sure that no one was watching or listening, that they thought FreshDirect was a good idea and they saw what I was trying to do, but they didn't dare get involved for fear that they'd be attacked too. As Martin Luther King Jr. said, "We will remember not the words of our enemies, but the silence of our friends."

Some of you out there either have or will experience this type of negativity from those you least expect: your own peers. It is very disturbing at the time it happens, but I promise you, it becomes less and less so as you just keep doing the work.

My advice to you is don't respond in kind and don't take it personally. Those who don't speak up are likely fearful of things that have nothing to do with you.

Forgive. You do not have to forget. It is always good to know who your friends aren't.

It was disappointing that our ability to focus FreshDirect on efforts to help it be a good corporate citizen was inhibited by having its focus drawn to the lawsuits brought on to stop the project by well-meaning pro bono legal professionals. FreshDirect reps felt that anything they did would be attacked by the activists, and they weren't wrong, so they were hesitant to try anything at all—even when we showed them that plenty of community residents supported them and would be willing to partner on mutually beneficial goals.

For example, we were unable to focus FreshDirect enough on creating opportunities for local food manufacturers to sell their products through FreshDirect's distribution system or advocate to build the infrastructure for cleaner truck fuels like compressed natural gas. Although CNG is a fossil fuel, it has significantly lower emissions, which is important because a chief issue in the South Bronx is pollution caused by the emissions from diesel fuels. I want all-electric vehicles everywhere all the time too, but diversifying what we have available now to reduce emissions until the renewable future arrives is also important.

We tried, but we were unable to convince the FreshDirect folks that the community was much bigger than a small group of activists suing them and spending way too much time on social media, but they were just too gun-shy to proceed. Despite all that, they did make good on their employment promises and developed some partnerships locally.

I was okay being the target so long as some good work got done.

A Phoenix Rising from the Ashes Is a Pretty Big Target

When you are doing something worthwhile, when you are breaking new ground, challenging the status quo wherever it is and wherever you are, you are going to upset someone. You have to learn to be comfortable with being uncomfortable.

I learned that lesson in the late 1990s, when I was a bright-eyed and bushy-tailed newbie within the community development and social justice world. I thought that it was a club in which everyone was welcomed and respected.

That was also when I first heard the Alana Davis cover of Ani DiFranco's feminist anthem, "32 Flavors." The image of a beautiful and powerful phoenix rising up from the ashes after a horrible death was the ultimate vision of transformation.

Alana Davis's burnished rendition had a catchy hook, and Ani DiFranco's lyrics were provocative. At the time, I thought of the song only in terms of romantic breakups.

But after I won a MacArthur Fellowship, the song took on a whole new meaning. I imagined the phoenix as it glided by, past the smoldering tension of jealous eyes. Suddenly, I was the phoenix. According to the MacArthur Foundation website, the John D. and Catherine T. MacArthur Fellowship provides "unrestricted fellowships to talented individuals who have shown extraordinary originality and dedication in their creative pursuits and a marked capacity for self-direction."[1] The year I won, the award came with a no-strings-attached $500,000 grant, released over five years.

Thanks to a highly secretive selection process, the awardees don't know that they've won until they get the call. Then they have to swear to keep the news private until all the awardees are contacted and the list is then released to the press.

Of course, I had heard of the MacArthur awards. The announcement always made the news. I thought it was a lovely thing for some brilliantly talented people. When I got the call, I assumed at first that I was being contacted to give a recommendation for any one of the many folks I knew who were MacArthur-level material.

It was a truly surreal time. There were countless congratulatory hugs, letters, emails, phone calls, cookies, and flowers from community members and well-wishers from around the world. I also had a few handfuls of experiences that gave me pause.

Some folks reacted to me in ways that made me believe that they thought the MacArthur I received was either undeserved or in some cases, rightfully theirs. Mind you, none of them were the ones I thought of as MacArthur level.

One community partner, a person I thought of as a friend until that moment, sent an email that said something like, "Congratulations on your award. I hope you'll never forget how you got where you are."

A few of my actual friends reported that other social justice activists had pulled them aside and questioned them about my authenticity, my worthiness, and how I was going to spend the money.

An ex-boyfriend (and not a good one) called to see if I would support his endeavors. I told him to write me a proposal. I never heard back from him, although I did chuckle to myself about what I would write in his rejection letter.

Online vandals began to maliciously edit my Wikipedia page with false and disparaging information.

And a few journalists who interviewed me shared that they had received unsolicited calls from activists warning them that I wasn't really from the community and certainly didn't represent the community.

A few days after the MacArthur announcement, I attended a meeting with about two dozen community activists from various organizations in the neighborhood. The discussion had already begun by the time I arrived.

As I walked in to take a seat, one of the attendees glared at me for a moment, then swept their eyes toward the rest of the group and stated emphatically, "Not all of us can get press like that." Some folks looked uncomfortable, but no one addressed the comment.

I knew there was tension. I could feel it. I left it alone too.

A few years later, I even had an order of protection filed against me by a person closely connected to people in that room. My crime? Saying hello to them in a "threatening manner."

Two police officers came to the coffee shop to issue the complaint. The white male cop was blushing and could barely look me in the eye. The Latina officer just sighed and said, "Could you just not speak when you see them coming?"

I was in the habit of being friendly to my neighbors, but I will admit, after that visit from the officers, I lavished even more overly cheerful greetings upon my complainant just because I thought they were being ridiculous.

Eventually, however, I realized that they could press charges if so inclined. I stopped acknowledging their presence, and they crossed the street when they saw me coming. I like to think of their detours as tacit acknowledgment that they know they are welcome to move if they find me unsettling, but I will go about my own business undeterred.

When I gave myself permission, I admitted I felt that I was the phoenix just gliding past.

Protest and Irony: People Will Hear What They Want to Hear

Despite the assertions of my detractors, I am, indeed, human.

It is never pleasant to have someone deny your humanity. But the reasons why it was denied seemed tragic and ironic.

We were protested on the day we were hosting a workshop for current and aspiring homeowners and small business owners within the area.

My company had taken advantage of two loan programs that supported both businesses and homeowners. We knew from our loan officers that they had a very low percentage of Bronxites applying for their products. We were eager to share these resources with the community at large because one of them provided low interest loans and the other provided 0 percent interest loans. You heard me: 0 percent.

We also had a guest speaker who was willing to talk to local property owners about how they could maximize the value of their property. As far as we were concerned, this was just a way to spread the word about generational wealth opportunities and new entrepreneurial development. However, it was clear that some didn't understand that.

Members of the fan club found a new ally. A decades-long member of the nonprofit industrial complex who had committed their professional life to "revitalizing" my community commented in a derogatory social media post about me. They referred to the workshop as my "latest effort to gentrify the community." As a result, the date of the fan club's proposed protest was rescheduled to coincide with the workshop.

Although I saw the post beforehand, I chose not to confront the person about it directly. Instead, I offered an olive branch.

We had known each other for years. I asked if we could give each other the benefit of the doubt and discuss whatever they felt was discomfiting about me and my work.

After what seemed like an eternity of the person's grunting absurdities such as "You know what it is. I shouldn't have to tell you," here's what I finally got from them:

> THEM: It's that self-gentrification.
> ME: What do you think it means?
> THEM: You know what it means!
> ME: I know what I meant, but what does it mean to you?
> THEM (*pointing at me*): It means when people like you grow up and go to college and then come back to stay.
> ME: What's the problem with that?
> THEM: What about all the other people that can't do that? What about the poor people?

Somehow or another, the Cinderella story of growing up in a downtrodden hood and clawing your way out to great success is an authentic representation of what should happen to the ones who had the capacity to make it out via education or career. Why were we not encouraged to stay and reinvest our hard-earned time and resources into the community that raised us?

So there I was, reclaiming my own neighborhood, and I was the problem.

What was it about my approach that was so threatening?

Why such very low expectations of the people the nonprofit industrial complex allegedly serves?

If I had a nickel for every time I heard some doctrinaire social justice enthusiast or philanthropic tool talk about "working themselves out of a job," I'd have at least two dollars and I would be able to point back to each and every one of them and see that they are in the same position they were in when I first heard them say it. Granted, they might be at another community organization or a different foundation, but they are essentially still doing the same thing and the people they "serve" seem stuck in a cycle of economic scarcity.

If their modus operandi is to advocate for the low-income people in the communities in which they worked, what would they do without them? What else would there be to focus on if they didn't have to manage poor people as they experienced their poverty?

That person and the indirect encouragement that their post provided my protesters was a shining example of misunderstanding one of my most often quoted statements: "If you want to be a part of the solution, engage the problem."

CHAPTER 15

SO WHAT *IS* THE PROBLEM?

To me, the problem was not that a monster named Gentrification came and destroyed and displaced everything in its path and replaced it with things for some wealthy White folks to come and enjoy. The end result of what people see and refer to as gentrification is a lot more subtle and complex than the rapacious monster some illustrate. The groundwork for gentrification is reinforced by those within the nonprofit industrial complex that operate with a distasteful attitude about people in low-status communities creating and retaining wealth.

In my observations, the nonprofit industrial complex has signaled that poverty is the more authentic state of being for people in low-status communities. Since they will always be needy with limited success in life, it's best to manage according to that principle. In the world of nonprofits, low income is associated with neighborhood preservation because poverty is mistakenly equated with culture.

The Impact of Limited Vision for Development in Low-Status communities

Two kinds of development are most common in low-status communities. The first is the aforementioned gentrification, in which the lower-income residents are replaced by those with higher incomes through a series of policy decisions, real estate projects, systemic racism, and predatory or discriminatory financial practices.

Gentrification is made especially noticeable when race is factored in. That would not be the case if we retained the successful minority residents. Economic levels would increase overall, but it shouldn't be considered "displacement" since residents didn't leave in the first place. Of course, the person who took umbrage at my staying in my own community would likely take issue with that statement.

We've dubbed the other type of real estate developed poverty-level economic maintenance (PLEM). Most folks nod in agreement when I list the types of developments that we would have characterized as such in low-status communities: the liquor stores, dollar stores, fast-food restaurants, check-cashing stores, pawn shops, and large concentrations of very low income subsidized affordable rental housing for the lowest income bands. There is money to be made in all of the above, but the overall assemblage of economic developments is not particularly inspiring for the local community and has the net effect of taking money out of the community.

Now, I'd like to think that most of those who are involved in community development in low-status communities are not willfully trying to make subpar projects. However, if PLEM projects are the vast majority of developments that happen in these communities, despite some other wonderful projects that may be happening nearby, the net result is persistent and concentrated poverty and, statistically, lower educational attainment, poor health outcomes, and higher rates of unemployment and incarceration.

Of course, people of color face historical inequities, in particular, reduced access to capital for homeownership and business development. However, one of the most awful consequences of the manifestation of systemic racism in real estate development in low-status communities is that many folks are selling because they have been led to believe that there is no value in their communities.

They often sell early and cheap and thus do not participate in the gains that happen in their former community. I know that firsthand because I couldn't convince my own siblings to hold on to our family home after our parents died. They appreciated my community mindedness, but they didn't believe that their old neighborhood was worth much.

In other words, just because you don't see value doesn't mean that others don't. Speculators prey on property owners in low-status communities who see only the blight that they are led to believe is in the community's DNA.

Let's assume that blight is not a part of the genetic makeup of low-status communities. Poverty is not a cultural attribute. The people from low-status communities are the keys to their own economic recovery.

As Dave Chappelle said in his 2020 special 8:46, "We're not desperate for heroes in the Black community."[1] It was an affirmation that greatness has always existed among us whether or not it was acknowledged, either by others or ourselves.

In my line of work, it's getting the heroes to stick around that's the challenge. I apply that same sentiment to low-status communities in general.

Some people cringe when they start to see doggie day cares and cute coffee shops appear in communities of color because they assume that these are White-owned and announce that what these places have on offer is not for them. However, I would like to state for the record that the first doggie day care in the South Bronx, Bronx Barx, was started by my friends and neighbors Renzo Pereda, a first-generation Peruvian American, and his husband, Steven Toledo, a second-generation Puerto Rican, born and raised in the South Bronx, *and* I heard that a hip-hop-themed coffee shop that serves wine, beer, and community pride was started by an awesome around-the-way girl I know too!

I would also like us to consider that gentrification doesn't happen when you start to see doggie day cares and cute coffee shops appear in communities of color. It happens when we tell ourselves that there is no value in our own communities and act accordingly.

A Third Type of Real Estate Development: Talent Retention

Some companies are legendary for the way they have tried to retain talent. A full day of the week to work on passion projects, stock options, paid transportation to and from work, free snacks, and ping pong tables in the hallways were just some of the perks offered.

Smart employers know they have to compete for talent. They work to create corporate cultures attractive enough to help ensure loyalty from their teams and encourage them not to leave.

Now imagine if a talent-retention approach was applied in low-status communities. These are communities in which the schools are worse, more environmental burdens are present, the air is more polluted, the parks and trees are fewer and less well-maintained, the health statistics are not good, and elected officials acknowledge these disparities as campaign tools but nothing really changes.

Low-status communities are places where inequality is assumed—both inside and outside those communities. They are inner cities, reservations, former Rust Belt towns with lots of White folks whose manufacturing jobs are long gone. Those of us born and raised in them are led to believe we should measure success by how far we get away from them, and those from outside looking in tend to treat those communities as problems with little hope of being solved, only managed.

If we looked at low-status communities like they were corporations and made it our business to keep the talent from leaving, we would have a different social and economic landscape in communities. Instead, we have a failure-retention model, and the well-intentioned efforts of activists, service providers, philanthropists, and government often serve to repel talent.

Despite the regulations and challenges, building subsidized low-income rental housing is a lucrative gig for developers, but it also entrenches a transient, landless class in low-status communities. Those people are essentially the equivalent of hourly low-wage earners in the community-as-corporation scenario.

Between the nonprofit and government sector and their engagement with community real estate development, there is relatively little talk of wealth creation versus programs designed to help people manage their lives in poverty. Most of their versions of community development leave no reason for successful people from these places to *want* to stay, and in most of the housing scenarios relegated to low-status communities, although most of these folks would not be considered rich, they make too much money to qualify for most affordable housing developments.

But what if we made *investments* in the future wealth-generating capacity of low-status community members? This includes projects such as housing and business development that address aspirations for their lives, complete with lifestyle infrastructure such as nice bars, cafes, and restaurants, as well as homeownership and local business development support for people who desire them. Those things are like company-paid health insurance or stock options to those hourly wage earners in our community-as-corporation idea. Company success equals individual success.

Currently, people who achieve individual success leave as soon as possible for the most part, which is *supported by the efforts* of activists, service providers, philanthropists, and government. And as I mentioned earlier, when these communities lose talent,

- They lose day-to-day consumer dollars that will allow better, and local businesses to launch and grow.
- They lose everyday examples of success, making it harder to teach the next generation.
- They lose reinvestment capital in the family home that their parents could buy in the past when property values were lower, because when they sell it, they eliminate any hope of passing that asset down to future generations.

I want to embolden people to take an approach that supports emotional well-being as well as economic wealth creation in low-status communities. We like nice things too.

CHAPTER 16

CONSTANT YEARNING

If you were Black in America during the 1970s, you were likely in front of the TV with your family whenever *Good Times* aired. This sitcom about the life and times of a family living in the housing projects on the South Side of Chicago ran for six seasons on a major network back when there were only a few channels to choose from: 133 episodes of us, seen in unison weekly over six years—no such thing as bingeing back then.

In one episode, called "The Windfall," James, the family patriarch played by the powerfully resolute John Amos, returned a bag that he found filled with $27,000 in cash that had been stolen in a heist from a local supermarket. His good deed was memorialized on the local news, when the owner of the supermarket chain promised him a large reward.

That "large" reward turned out to be a $50 gift certificate at the supermarket—predictable given the store owner's miserly reputation. All the residents knew the groceries were overpriced anyway.

During the climax of the episode, the audience learns that James didn't return *all* of the money. Esther Rolle played his wife, Florida, and she chastised him for holding back $2,000.

FLORIDA: Honey, we get by.
JAMES: I am tired of getting by! I want to get over![1]

Ultimately, James did return all the money.

James was the epitome of strength and honor to me. I could tell he loved his family deeply and was disappointed that he couldn't provide more for them. It also helped that he looked like my own dad.

I was only eight or nine but I certainly knew James was experiencing a moral conundrum. He and his family lived in the ghetto, and he took care of them as best he could with his working two jobs. Florida worked too whenever she could find a job.

I knew James didn't *want* to steal and that all he wanted was for his family to not just survive, but thrive. Deep inside, I understood that.

I've been fascinated with that *Good Times* episode for decades. I loved James and his unrelenting commitment to his family, and I was angry at how the owner of the grocery chain undervalued James's good deed. But I always felt, even as a kid when I first saw that episode, that both of the roles the male actors played were based on default attitudes and practices assumed in communities like the Chicago's South Side:

- Poor folks will always be in desperate need, and there will always be those who know how to and will profit off of them.
- Even a father's devotion to supporting his family can be tarred by the brush of illegitimacy and pettiness.

I didn't like that one bit. I still don't. So I find myself asking the question that James might have asked himself: why can't we thrive in our own communities?

Concentrating Poverty = Exacerbated Inequality

Poverty continues because structures are in place and supported to continue its cycle. For example, when new housing is being built in an American low-status community, it is almost exclusively "affordable" housing—code for low-income rental housing. Lawmakers, activists, and real estate developers agree that it's a good thing. Mixed-income housing is an orphan among advocates.

However, statistically, when there is a concentration of low-income rental housing, there is an attendant concentration of all the other issues associated with poverty, including poor health outcomes, low educational attainment, families affected by the impacts of a family member involved in the justice system, higher unemployment, and lower incomes.

In New York City, for example, the de Blasio mayoral administration, the one that declared itself as one of the most progressive in the city's history, proudly announced its target for building three hundred thousand new units of affordable housing. Nearly all the units were reserved for New York City's lowest income residents and located in the city's poorest neighborhoods.

I had the opportunity to ask the mayor if his administration was aware of the impact that the continued concentration of poverty already had in impoverished neighborhoods. I knew that campaign contributors from the real estate industry and grassroots advocates were both supportive of policies that statistics showed would ultimately result in greater social costs down the line—even if from different motivations.

The mayor agreed that concentrating more poor people in poor neighborhoods had the net effect of exacerbating the costly social issues that were already there. He shared with me that he was personally very supportive of mixed-income housing and commercial development as a strategy to increase community stability in low-income communities.

He continued, noting that he had two constituencies that usually didn't agree on anything, and they both wanted the same thing:

1. Activists wanted more affordable housing to be built for the most economically vulnerable, and that was assumed to be rental apartments.
2. Real estate developers wanted more low-income rental housing to be built because they knew how to work the affordable

rental subsidy and other financing systems and make some-
what lower but still very low-risk returns.

So, he asked, what else could a mayor do? I reminded him that
his administration had recently passed on an opportunity to show the
very type of leadership that he was asking about.

How the Government Maintains the Status Quo in Low-Status Communities

Years earlier, I had brought to the city's attention the possibility of
using a vacant city-owned property with a tormented history to create
the kind of economically vibrant and diverse development that would
signal a new era for low-status communities around the country.

One day in early 2011, I was walking to work from my house on
Manida Street, which was across the street from the house I grew up in.
As I crossed Spofford Avenue and looked to my left to avoid oncoming
traffic, less than a block away from me was a sight that I had seen from
my earliest days—the sign for the Spofford Juvenile Detention Center.

Opened in the 1950s on a five-acre site, the center housed over
a thousand young people at its height. Spofford had been recently
closed, due in large part to the successful efforts of children's rights
and prison reform advocates.

The building was a threatening boogeyman in our community.
Parents would tell kids that they would end up there if they didn't act
right. It really was a bad place that broke children before they had a
chance to grow.

My father was a janitor there in the 1970s. Awful conditions common in juvenile justice facilities persisted there. I remember hearing
him tell my mom that he wished our house was bigger so we could take
in some of those kids. Some were placed there because of the things
their parents might have done. Overall, the children were treated like
adult criminals. Rehabilitation was not the goal; punishment was. My
father knew that all of those kids would be portrayed as the monsters
that the media loved to hate.

Walking to my office that morning in 2011, I didn't just see the big, ghostly white brick shell of a boogeyman building that I normally saw. This time, I saw possibilities. I knew that it could be a place where we would be able to demonstrate at scale a model for mixed-income housing and mixed-use commercial development with the power to transform a chronically underperforming community.

I knew in my core that there was a market for economically diverse communities that meet the needs and desires of an economically diverse group of people. I was excited about the possibility and immediately started triangulating the people I knew within city government who might be supportive of, or at the very least, interested in, the kind of transformational real estate development that our city desperately needed in low-status communities and help move this ball down the field.

Mathew Wambua was commissioner for the New York City Department of Housing Preservation and Development in 2011 and was willing to set a meeting with me for six weeks out—just enough time to secure other resources I needed.

I then put the call out to architecture firms in my network, and Scott Schiamberg and Anthony Fieldman, then at Perkins+Will, took us on—donating a substantial level of service to help create a conceptual design for the future of Spofford to be used in the meeting with Commissioner Wambua (which they also hosted in their beautiful offices for me). Both Anthony and Scott have moved on from P+W, but I remain close to them both.

Together, we produced an insightful concept for a different direction in housing and economic policy for low-status communities, and thankfully, it captured the imagination of Commissioner Wambua and his team too. The commissioner's only concern was that the site was not under his department's jurisdiction, but that of the New York City Administration for Children's Services (ACS). After he explored a bit deeper, it was apparent that ACS's primary concern was that any plan needed to include a meaningful amount of "supportive housing," such as housing for youth aging out of foster care, grandparent housing, or something similar.

A multiagency task force was created to assess possibilities for a transformed Spofford. However, the Bloomberg mayoral administration was drawing to a close, and a project of this scale could not progress to the next stage given the shrinking window of opportunity leading up to the first change of mayoral administrations in twelve years.

Not wanting to let the fire go out, we spent the next several years working to keep the idea of Spofford redevelopment in the public eye and the city's mind.

How Does Information Travel?

After the FreshDirect saga—in our opinion, a good idea that was communicated poorly by the city—we had to salvage the wreckage instead of building beyond expectations. We knew a better way to communicate ideas around community development was needed. Community members tend to appreciate a reliable stream of information and opportunities for feedback.

Community organizations come in all shapes and sizes, but they often attract a similar crowd and create a dynamic that makes some people feel excluded for a huge variety of reasons. It's just the clique dynamic, and it can happen very easily.

We wanted to solve the barriers that were keeping smart, dynamic, longtime community members away from the existing community organizations and local government. We also wanted to improve the quality of information gathering and distribution.

Melissa Lomba, US Air Force reservist who was born in Puerto Rico and had lived in the South Bronx since she was eight, was our COO. She initiated the Hunts Point Advisory Board (HPAB) made up of nontraditional leaders in the community. She felt that a network like this would help prevent misinterpretations about our projects and teach us a lot in the process too. I agreed!

Her plan was to facilitate feedback venues to collect opinions, real concerns among the pivotal community members, and generate fresh ideas and perspectives. The HPAB brought together disparate voices within the geographic area comprising business owners, residents, and informal networks of local influencers who did not generally fall within the usual cast of characters that the nonprofit industrial complex looks for but were deeply entrenched in the community and highly regarded by many.

We settled on buffet dinners with ample supplies of wine hosted twice a month. The lightly catered biweekly forums allowed a safe venue for informal leaders of the community to express their opinions, build projects together, avoid organizational funding pressures or other agendas, and sometimes just vent! It allowed for critical exchanges regarding projects or issues that each member was welcomed to bring to the board.

It became a repeating and very valuable pattern:

1. Meet on a biweekly basis.
2. Identify problems within or that affect our community.
3. Compile and document the problems and provide recommendations to alleviate or eliminate them.
4. Research city agencies and key players that can help.
5. Ask for volunteers to appear at the pivotal meetings wearing matching red HPAB polo shirts, where agencies and key players would notice.
6. Ensure that all points in our documented recommendations are addressed and that each point on the recommendations list is brought up and discussed to our satisfaction.
7. Continue to show up and respectfully address our concerns until we see that our voices have been heard and we have received commitment to act on identified issues.
8. Follow up.
9. Identify new issues, challenges, concerns, and solutions.
10. Repeat.

The HPAB helped design and disseminate community needs/aspiration surveys that eventually garnered more than five hundred responses. The results of that project are infused in our approach to the talent-retention strategy that informs all our real estate work. They also provided critical information about community ambitions that encouraged us to start a tech social enterprise as well as the cafe.

The HPAB chose several initiatives to focus on. Here is an abridged list of their accomplishments in 2013–15:

Street/Sidewalk Lighting
    Problem Identified: There was a need to bring awareness to street lighting and transportation issues at every city Department of Transportation "Vision Zero" meeting.
    Outcome: The DOT replaced Hunts Point lights and placed new ones on Lafayette Avenue and in other identified areas.

Rikers Island Crime Statistics Included with Local 41st Precinct District
    Problem Identified: Insurance rates and property values were negatively affected.
    Outcome: Crime statistics districts were redrawn, and statistics were decoupled.

BronxWorks Homeless Shelter
    Problem Identified: There was a need to clean up trash, reduce public loitering and open drug usage, and increase the safety of the immediate area of Lafayette Avenue and Barretto Street related to the BronxWorks shelter.
    Outcome: Increased vigilance and new policies implemented by facility administration, greater vigilance from the New York Police Department (NYPD), and new lighting by the DOT in the area resulted in increased overall safety and a decrease in crime.

Sanitation Issues
    Problem Identified: The launch of a 311 call-in campaign led to reports of all sorts of sanitation issues (over 240 tickets filed).

Outcome: The city council allocated funds for bimonthly Hunts Point median maintenance, as well as daily sidewalk cleaning.

Prostitution

Problem Identified: Prostitutes frequented Lafayette Avenue.

Outcome: Prostitutes were no longer seen on the avenue due to increased NYPD enforcement.

Dog Poo Concerns

Problem Identified: Dog poo was left on sidewalks.

Outcome: Majora Carter Group, LLC, sponsored bilingual signage "Pick It Up/Limpia Lo," free to community members to put up on private properties. No current legislation exists to fine violators—unless directly observed by the NYPD.

In addition to the HPAB members' self-directed initiatives, they provided critical intel to us that helped our projects reflect community aspirations. They were very involved in the Spofford redevelopment planning and communication. For example, upon the suggestion of HPAB members, we hosted poetry and theater projects in which members wrote and performed poems based on their personal experiences with the community, as well as a play about Spofford.

We also partnered with the software company Autodesk and used the reimagining of the Spofford site as the basis for an international design competition.[2] Autodesk sponsored an event with food and wine at StartUp Box (our tech social enterprise) on a busy corner that transformed our storefront headquarters on the main commercial street in our South Bronx community into a gallery for the award-winning entrants.

One attendee was Yusuf Salaam. He was one of the alleged "Central Park Five," the young men who were infamously and wrongfully convicted in 1990 of brutally assaulting and raping a white female jogger in Central Park.

The Central Park Five had recently been awarded a multimillion-dollar settlement from the city of New York because of the wrongful conviction and years they had all spent behind bars, including some of them at Spofford. Yusuf looked at the designs produced for the competition and mused that it was time for Spofford to be no more.

After two years on the shelf with no action whatsoever, Spofford was put back on the radar in late 2014 when the administration released a Request for Expressions of Interest (RFEI) to gather ideas for the future of the site. I was happily surprised to see that the specific language and concepts we designed and used for our initial meeting with Commissioner Wambua (which became the Autodesk international design competition rules), and broadcast via numerous presentations were directly reflected in the RFEI. The typical business-as-usual approach to government housing policy in low-status communities wasn't in the RFEI, but concepts such as strategic mixed-income housing *and* mixed-used commercial development had seeped their way into this RFEI across several years, new commissioners, and a new administration.

The RFEI was an open call for new ideas that could meet the goals we had outlined, using methods we had defined that meet people where they are today with an eye on how far they can go tomorrow: economic diversity, brain-drain reduction, and progressive business development. Of course, we submitted not just a plan but an extremely well-crafted proposal.

The team I had assembled was incredibly accomplished and was composed of more minority- and women-owned firms than New York City had ever seen together on one project team. And out of the six partner companies on our team, two were led by White men because we value diversity.

Our proposal included one hundred units for low-income homeowners, eight hundred units of low- to medium-income homes, and three hundred units of market rate rentals.

We included more than fifty units for young people aging out of foster care as our supportive housing component. Many young people that age out of foster care become homeless by the time they are thirty years old, in large part due to their not being able to create meaningful attachments during their formative years. Ours was an integrated approach that placed their apartments and support resources throughout the complex instead of isolating them in a group home type of environment.

We also had an economic development plan for local and national businesses that would have resulted in more than seven hundred permanent jobs.

The city stayed in familiar territory and chose to award the site to a pair of White male-led development companies to build a typical low-income housing project. Some of the commercial tenants included in their proposal were fictitious, and their largest tenants were community centers and health clinics.

Through that project, the "most progressive" of all New York City mayoral administrations actively maintained the status quo, which is well known to create more problems and social cost obligations, in one of the poorest neighborhoods in the city.

CHAPTER 17

THE ILLUSION OF A PERFECT OPPORTUNITY

Regardless of how wonderful and impactful a vision for a community development might be, those entrenched in playing and winning at political machinations would never stick their necks out in support of a vision that could affect the favors they might need one day. I learned that the hard way.

A Rude Awakening

We set up the conditions to put the redevelopment of Spofford on the city's radar, but we didn't know to look behind the curtain. I truly believed my hard work and accomplishments would count for something, and they did, but only if I moved in one direction.

A girl from the hood who got some breaks and was working to make her hood a better place? Fine for a park—not redevelopment projects in the range of hundreds of millions.

I was naive in assuming that my great city was serious about expanding the type of people who got the privilege to develop here. I certainly believed all the research that stated that diversity in companies led to greater innovation and profits. Of course, I figured my great city believed that too.

I was far too trusting to believe that the real estate industry, the city, and the nonprofit world would allow a pitiful repeat of what had already been done before. Their worldview did not include someone like me popping up and saying business as usual was problematic, and maybe we should try something new.

A few HPAB members were in attendance when a city representative informally announced at a community meeting that a development team led by two White males had been chosen to redevelop Spofford. The city had made the decision without discussion with the larger community and, specifically, without the HPAB folks, who had been quite open that they had been working for years to align a plan that was feasible, community led, and yes, riskier because it was far more aspirational than the usual low expectations that the city usually had for development within the community.

The HPAB members were horrified but bounced back and led an effort to understand why the city chose such an uninspiring proposal: no homeownership, no housing diversity, and phony "economic development." The chosen proposal had made-up fictitious businesses listed as anchor tenants, such as "Hunts Point Brewery," instead of the real businesses that the HPAB had helped recruit.

Looking back, I realized I had lost the game before I even entered.

The project was awarded to a team that donated heavily to the current mayoral campaign. One of the leads was an out-of-state construction company that had anti-labor allegations levied against them on a regular basis. Redeveloping Spofford would be their first project as a developer in New York City.

Yes, I had put the idea on the table. I was very up-front about our ambitious plan. I presented it in lectures around the world to the press, to agencies, and of course, to my neighbors.

I honestly thought I had a shot based on our open and transparent process, diverse constituency, and positivity. I had hoped that even if we didn't win, the city would choose a project that was better than ours. It still would have been a hard pill to swallow, but I would have absolutely been okay with that outcome.

To put a personally tragic cherry on top, news of the city's choice for the Spofford redevelopment team was released to the public on October 27, 2016, my fiftieth birthday. I was booked to deliver a talk for a business group in Troy, New York. My husband drove and I cried sporadically for most of the drive up there, sucked it up for the actual lecture, and shed more tears on the way back home. All I wanted to do was crawl into bed with a dose of the generic version of ZzzQuil that I picked up at a truck stop and sleep it off for a while.

When we arrived home, my sister Jackie, her daughter and one of my best friends, Njeri, and a friend who was staying with us at the time greeted us at our house with balloons and a cake to celebrate my birthday. James thought it would lift my spirits. Bless his heart.

I know they all meant well. I pretended to appreciate their efforts, although I am not sure if I was convincing. No, I am positive I was not convincing.

It took a while, but now I can laugh at that girl that was me. I now know the game was not meant for me to win at that time.

I had surrounded myself with a team that was not only successful and proven but they were mostly women- and minority-led firms! I wasn't connected to the industry and played no role in getting people elected or advanced politically. When you are trying to make a deal with a city, that is the capital respected. The local people we connected with on the ground, despite their numbers and the organized information-gathering power we had assembled, were of no value to anyone in this equation—except me, and I didn't count.

The Club

When I decided I was going to be a real estate developer, there wasn't much of a welcome wagon of people I knew in the industry waiting to take me under their wing.

There have been some notable exceptions: Carlton Brown, a Jackson, Mississippi–born Black developer who pioneered "green" housing long before it became a buzzword, and Kathyrn Wylde, one of the most powerful women in New York City, who was the first to encourage me to consider myself a real estate developer. They have both been great supporters in their own way.

However, even my earliest attempts to break into development were viewed with suspicion.

Our very first project was to redevelop a two-family home, two blocks away from the one we already owned. The loan officer questioned why I wanted to purchase an investment property in my own community since I "had *one* already!" She was certain that the underwriters would require "more clarification" as to why I needed another property.

She instructed me to write a letter stating that I was a community-minded person who needed more space because we planned to become foster parents. That was true, but she advised me not to put anything in the letter about our investment or development goals.

I wondered how many White applicants would be asked the questions she asked of me. I bet she didn't make any of them write a letter indicating why they were good citizens as she negated their business goals.

But yes, I wrote that letter.

Over the years, my work led me to meet many of the major players in New York City sustainability and the real estate industry at events and networks where my projects and perspective were being awarded and applauded with great enthusiasm. These were the so-called opportunities and powerful networks denied to people of color historically. But when I wanted to negotiate a piece of the deal and not simply play an unremunerated "community partner" role, my interests were somehow questioned.

One evening, I found myself up on a stage for a panel in a packed auditorium to kick off a museum's retrospective of Robert Moses, aka the "master builder," whose grand schemes to remanufacture the landscape of New York State came at the expense of many poor communities of color, including my own.

Ironically, it was also the first day of Black History Month! This set a stage for me and came with a challenging burden that I was proud but honestly very nervous to take on. I was last in line to speak after all the big guys each had their moment. If this were a baseball analogy, I hit it out of the park: applause lines, spontaneous exclamations of support, standing ovation.

The most noted speaker on the panel that night was a very powerful deputy mayor. I knew that the things I had to say would challenge some of his policies and beliefs, but they had to be said and I hoped that this would open doors for greater dialogue. I believed he might see and even work with me to deploy my value toward our shared goals for the city's future with the resources at his disposal, but he did not behave that way.

Within days after the panel, I learned I was instead effectively blacklisted throughout his and even adjacent city government agencies, all because of a damaged ego one night in a stuffy auditorium. With all the advantages both his position and privilege afforded him, a literal poor Black girl from the ghetto was some kind of threat to be shut out. A barrier arose between me and all those channels of government and development that needed what I had to offer, and the fear in its wake lasted for over a decade after that man and the administration he served had moved on. That's how fragile your position can be in this world.

Another example is after that we lost the Spofford project (but before I truly understood that the game was rigged), I assumed that we would work with our partners together on other projects in the future. These were long-term legit players in the game and among the handful of real estate developers in the city that frequently won major projects like this one. They knew that after the dust cleared on Spofford, there would be plenty of other projects to work on, so they could easily let this one slide. There was no reason for them to align themselves with some uppity negress who possessed nothing our city government valued.

Successful developers like them had no incentive to bite the hand that fed them, so they moved on quickly and without pretense.

I should have known something was up when one of my colleagues told me that they were approached by a young White male associate from one of my partners' teams. This young guy and his friend (another White male who worked at the city), who were part of the team that rejected our proposal, complained that I'd been talking to the press about the city's opaque selection process.

I had been talking to the press about the potential of a transformational project at Spofford for *five* years, long before any of them had even considered it. I've been an international thought leader in community revitalization for nearly two decades, while those two boys were barely out of college. I had shared my concerns that the city lost an opportunity to do something different and special, and these two young White males were compelled, reflexively, to tattle on me.

After diplomatically illustrating to their bosses how their behavior was cowardly, gossipy, inappropriate, and likely sexist and racist at its core, I figured we were all grown-ups and would use this incident as a teachable moment. Nope. Future efforts I made to partner with them were met with silence.

I know. I told you I was too trusting and naive at times.

I bring up these examples to help us all identify where we fall in this destructive continuum of power, race, gender, and money. I don't exactly know how to solve these forces in American society, but I am grateful I can now see things that I couldn't see before and share what is going on so we can hopefully change it. Along the way, people whom we believe are friends, mentors, mentees, and even partners on major projects can disappoint us, often gravely.

Reclaiming your community can come at costs like these to individuals in many contexts. Knowing if you are playing a detrimental or beneficial role in their quest for equality and progress is not always clear but critical for us to heal as a nation and for the world.

Membership Denied

At every turn, roadblocks prevented me from being accepted into a club that didn't have many members like me.

We naively assumed that if our local politicians recognized our organized, cogent, future-facing approach, they would champion the cause for the hometown team. I overestimated and misunderstood the power of local elected officials.

I'll never know if they were beholden to or afraid of forces larger than their limited powers and vision could summon. Or if they did try to help, they were unwilling, or simply had little to offer. Either way, they were not going to stick their necks out in support of a vision that could affect their reelection chances or political favors they might need one day. It was as if the organized opinions and aspirations of the many don't hold up to the dealmaking by the few. And, within that few, nonprofit industrial complex players sit comfortably.

There's always a supply of reliable community groups that allow the political and agency folks the ability to claim "outreach." Those community partners are handpicked and gathered behind the scenes to show that a project has community "support." In exchange for their cooperation, they get discounted rental space for a number of years or maybe a contribution to their efforts, but any "equity" is in name only, not an actual part of the deal.

When I asked one of them what percentage of equity they were getting from the deal, they looked at me as if I'd suggested they should eat their own children: "We're doing this to provide a service for the community, not for the money!" "You think these White boys running this show are doing this because they care? They are doing it for the money and are happy that 'community partners' don't expect to be in on their deal." Then they abruptly ended our meeting. There I go, making friends again.

I really do hope that that person was defensive because I scratched too close to the surface and maybe their organization did have some equity. Or maybe they just felt stupid because they didn't even know to ask for equity. I hope it was the former.

It seemed that as long as I stayed within the familiar territory of "community activist," being my beautiful Black and female self didn't work against me. Venturing outside that lane and into the realm of development was where political access was needed to make deals happen.

It took a long time for me to accept that some were trying to weaken my resolve to keep on that path. It took me only a little while to understand why.

Strange Bedfellows

When the nonprofit industrial complex is working well in low-status communities, activists, government agencies, and philanthropists robotically sing the same dirge, heralding their preferred default development attributes that have been sung for decades.

Here's what it looks like:

+   Low-income rental housing, usually with space reserved for a community center.
+   A plethora of programs for poor people allegedly designed to help move them out of poverty. Such programs are proposed and executed by various nonprofit actors (the ones from outside the community are consistently funded at levels much higher than local activists') or city agencies and supported by philanthropic or public funds.
+   A static poverty rate. Although the rate doesn't budge, more of the same type of programs are spawned year after year.

In the background, you'll hear them cheerlead, individually or collectively, for an array of programs designed to promote change, complete with lots of conversations, town halls, white papers, and conferences on topics like community land trusts, which take years to produce (most rarely move beyond the planning phase) while dozens of normal real estate deals fly through and thousands of Black- and Brown-owned properties are sold off to outside interests.

Maintaining the status quo in low-status communities seems to hold some kind of appeal for those very disparate groups. Although some of them might consider themselves at odds with each other most of the time, I've always found it curious that they seem to support the same kind of development. However, if overall these status quo projects are the only ones that happen in these communities, despite some other wonderful projects happening nearby, the net result is continued, concentrated poverty and the attendant health, educational, environmental, and justice issues statistically associated with high poverty communities.

The poverty-level economic maintenance found in low-status communities appears in familiar forms: pawn shops, check-cashing stores, fast-food restaurants, pharmacies, health clinics, and large amounts of subsidized rental housing. This chorus of economic vultures circles around low-status communities because there is money to be made—but those dollars do not circulate back into the local economy. Are those businesses locally owned? Do they generate a sense of pride in one's community?

Those types of places are the architecture of low expectations. This landscape reminds people, and their dollars, that there is more to aspire to outside of where you are right now.

Without notable, beautiful, soul-soothing, wealth-generating places that make people feel like they don't have to move out of their neighborhood to live in a better one, people leave.

Brain drain doesn't just happen in the developing world. Low status American communities have experienced it for generations now. This outward migration helps continue the shameful American legacy of treating those communities as collateral damage in a game that enriches a small number of outsiders.

What the Game Looks Like

The first time we had a consultant map out a financial plan for a project we wanted to build, I knew the basics about loans and that various city, state, and federal programs subsidized building costs for lower-income housing. What I did not know were the ways and the amounts developers got paid on these projects.

For instance, we specced a new mixed-use project with 150 units of housing as well as commercial space that would cost about $75 million to build over a couple of years. To cover our overhead and expenses, we figured we would require about a million dollars. It seemed fair considering the amount of work we'd have to do and the team we'd have to bring on.

My husband and I were on a conference call with our consultant to go over the budget. We saw a line item called "developer fee" to the tune of $9 million.

"Crap," I thought. "Is that cash equity we'll be expected to put in? How are we going to do that?"

Our consultant explained with an apologetic tone that some of that developer fee would be deferred until after the building was occupied. The fee itself was smaller than it usually would be because, as we directed, they steered clear of 100 percent low-income affordable units and included a healthy portion of market-rate units.

In other words, because we wanted a more diverse income mix as per our talent-retention real estate strategy, we would lose access to substantial subsidy dollars because the farther you went up the income ladder, the less the subsidy programs paid.

I put our consultant on hold. James and I looked at each without blinking, mouths agape.

"That's how much these guys make?" I blurted out.

"No wonder they do this!" James exclaimed. Once we composed ourselves, we went back on the call.

That's when I understood why the world of affordable real estate development was such a jealously guarded society in which only the privileged few were allowed entry, with dedicated support by their allies within city, state, and federal agencies. It was also clear to me that most activists really had no idea about how much money they were unlocking for these guys to support their own lifestyles. Otherwise, why would they advocate so vociferously for the construction of housing that historically and primarily benefited the builders of the housing more than the people who lived in it?

In many cases, once the subsidy term ended, the buildings' owners or management were under no obligation to keep those buildings affordable to low-income tenants. For example, low-income rental buildings that were constructed under New York State's Mitchell-Lama program with low-interest mortgages are allowed to be taken out of the program after twenty years, and landlords can offer units for market rate.

And thus, desperation for more units of affordable housing is a cycle that never ends.

Our Racist Economic History Keeps Repeating Itself

President Franklin D. Roosevelt's New Deal was a series of programs, financial reforms, and public works projects that were designed to help Americans recover from the Great Depression. In the long term, it set a precedent for the government to play a greater role in the social and economic interests of citizens.

Roosevelt had a problem getting the New Deal passed in Congress. Racist Southern congressmen would not let it happen if any wealth-creating benefits were extended to Blacks. FDR capitulated. The impacts of this move are felt to this day as evidenced by the consistently widening wealth gap between Black and White Americans.

Through the Fair Housing Administration, the New Deal severely limited access to capital for homeownership and business development by Black Americans. It set the foundation for major public policies affecting housing segregation and lending discrimination that have been built on the manifestation of that White supremacist ideology.

Later on, it set the foundation for government policy to subsidize affordable housing development that, for all intents and purposes, further economically, socially, and of course, racially segregated and disadvantaged the Black community in America.

Some of America's largest real estate developers profit nicely from the affordable housing system.[1] Some of the biggest got their start building the types of public housing that are now deemed some of the worst in the country.

Interestingly, much of the legislation behind those subsidies was originally designed so that low-income housing would be built in "high opportunity areas," enabling low-income residents to have their children educated in safe neighborhoods with good schools and other resources. However, almost none of the subsidies were ever used that way.

"High opportunity areas" is community development parlance for wealthier and Whiter neighborhoods with good schools and other community resources. The people who already lived in high opportunity areas wanted none of those low-income families in their neighborhoods, especially if they were Black.

White supremacist ideals molded the infrastructure that limited Black Americans' ability to acquire and retain wealth in our country for generations. It was also very effective in making people of color buy into the idea that our communities would never truly thrive, so we had to prepare for an inevitable life of low expectations within our communities.

What We Don't Know Can't Help Us

I've been called many choice words by some activists within the social justice industrial complex, but "gentrifier" seems to be one of their favorites.

I practice an approach to real estate development that increases economic diversity in low-status communities from the inside out. However, despite my often-stated goal of using real estate development to decrease the wealth gap and improve the quality of life in low-status communities, all they hear is "real estate development," which in their world seems equivalent to a demonic force.

They are staunch advocates for the construction of more low-income affordable housing and homeless shelters. Period.

Once I received a call from the campaign office of a candidate for a local office. I asked repeatedly about the candidate's position on supporting low-income homeowners in the area to keep their homes. The campaigner on the phone got heated and screamed at me: "What about the people who don't own homes? What about them? Have you thought about *that*?"

I politely stated that my question did not imply that those people were unimportant. However, the constituency of owners had been so thoroughly diminished that this pivotal class of minority families were not seen as a part of anyone's interest to advocate for.

It was easy for candidates to push subsidized rental housing as a way to protect residents from the onslaught of gentrification. However, many people are unaware that the paths to subsidizing these projects are really only accessible to developers with plenty of cash on hand, patience, and high taxes they want to avoid on big profits from their market-rate deals. Other rules, limits, and minimums effectively keep out anyone on the way up from tapping these rivers of government cash (the people's money) to make the kind of waves that someone new could bring to the industry.

The volunteer espousing a main point of their candidate's platform was not unique, although I suggested to them that yelling at a known serial voter wasn't a best practice.

That exchange did make me recall the conversation I had with the mayor years earlier, when he said affordable housing real estate developers and low-income housing advocates both wanted the same thing. Despite the regulations and challenges, subsidized low-income rental housing is not a bad deal for developers, and low-income people do need affordable housing.

Economic benefits disproportionately accrue to the developers whether or not they make a good product. Incentive to improve the quality of life for the residents is not part of their deal—it's hard to put that in a deal unless the developer already has the right insight and wants to do it.

Granted, not all affordable housing developers are terrible, but it is a very small and primarily homogeneous group, the cost of entry into the industry is very high, and the environment of racial exclusion has stifled creativity in terms of urban design and innovation in this sector of the economy and most others too.

Real estate development could be a transformational tool to support racial equality and diversity within the real estate industry and more equitable community development, but the industry overall is not acknowledging, let alone leading, in any of these important areas. That's why we need a diverse ecosystem of developers with different sensitivities to how people want to live.

The Devil You Know Is Less Scary Than the Devil You Don't

I do understand the well-founded suspicion around the changes that people see happening in low-status communities. Even if the changes were desired for decades, when they start to come, people reflexively fear that these improvements must be for someone else. Public safety, cleaner streets, and better housing, stores, and services are all suspect.

Fear of change seems entrenched within the methodology of the nonprofit industrial complex overall, wherein low incomes and neighborhood preservation are morosely linked. In turn, poverty is mistakenly equated with culture through programs and projects that cater to people stuck in the cycle of poverty within low-status communities, such as food banks and rental housing assistance, versus programs designed to improve their economic well-being, such as financial literacy, credit repair, homeowner stabilization, and local entrepreneurial development.

Preserving poverty and calling it "culture" assumes that people remaining in a low-status community will never be successful and that they are the only "authentic" representatives of those areas. If they are successful, it indicates that they don't really belong there or are somehow "inauthentic." Statistically, those communities are examples of gross inequalities pervasive throughout our country, so let's not build projects that preserve the policy mistakes going back to FDR's administration, which in turn were echoes of slavery.

We saw the problem of status quo development as part of my consulting and real estate practice. I don't presume much; I launch ideas in an observable context. I want to broaden the idea of who should do development and expand an approach that creates reasons for emotional and economic wealth creation in low-status communities and is designed to retain talent, not repel it.

I recognize that our approach to real estate development is unorthodox, controversial even, and definitely higher risk. And I am hardly the default developer. I'm a Black woman actually from a low-status community, so I understand that my presence in the field is confusing at best, threatening at worst.

Our work focuses on executing projects that no one expects to see happen in low-status communities in advance of a typical real estate development curve. Our mission is for low-status community members to experience a great community that meets their needs as well as their aspirations while they are ever more successful in it. Why is this a problem?

CHAPTER 18

REAL-LIFE EXAMPLES FORM
A NEW NARRATIVE

The world may be filled with lots of naysayers, but it also has plenty of amazing people who see hope and possibility where others see only barriers. Vibrant and viable alternatives to the status quo development that is usually reserved for American low-status communities do exist.

However, *trusting* that low-status community members can be intimately involved in the development of their own communities is too great a psychological leap for many both inside and outside of American low-status communities.

How can we embrace the risk of capital and competitiveness as well as have the faith to believe that many more are capable of succeeding than we see today?

Capitalism as a Tool to Gentrify Your Own Community

In 2019, Shawn Corey Carter, better known as Jay-Z, freestyled a rap in a tribute to his late friend Nipsey Hussle, the South Los Angeles–born-and-raised rapper, philanthropist, and entrepreneur known for using economic developments to revitalize his hometown.

Nipsey was well known and loved for how he invested in and provided opportunities for his community. He purchased a shopping center in South Los Angeles so that small local businesses could set up shop there and launched a coworking space and STEM project.

He also owned Marathon Clothing, the flagship store for his clothing line, which delivered jobs and local pride to his South Los Angeles neighborhood. Nipsey was gunned down in its parking lot, apparently because of a personal grievance.

At Nipsey Hussle's memorial service, Jay-Z paid homage to Nipsey's dedication to economically empowering his own community. Jay-Z used the moment as a rallying cry for Black folks to empower their own communities from the inside out and break free from the crabs-in-a-barrel mentality by supporting each other and remaining attached to those behind as you peek over the barrel's edge.

But what made folks' heads spin around was when he encouraged us to gentrify our own hoods for ourselves before others come in and do it to us.

Like any good piece of art, it prompted debate and discussion. The word "gentrify" clearly garnered the most controversy.[1]

To some, the word provoked a viscerally negative response associated with the wholesale and violent displacement of people of color from what they would define as their own communities. Others saw the phrasing as a call for economic revitalization to be done by local community members.

However, as I learned firsthand, for many people, the word is far too triggering to promote any kind of useful discussion about wealth creation or community economic development in low-status communities. Ensuing discussions tend to center more on the word itself rather than the intents, purposes, and plans for the future.

So the fact that I had added "self-" in front of the term to refer to development that is "by us and for us" was often overlooked when I started flying it out there after I met with Dr. Ronald Carter, former president of Johnson C. Smith University, who coined the term "self-gentrification" to describe how capital had been directed toward local developers to revitalize the distressed neighborhood adjacent to his HBCU in Charlotte, North Carolina.

A world-famous businessman and musician and the president of an acclaimed HBCU (both named Carter and no relation to me that I know of) both caught a lot of heat for using the G-word to highlight the extraordinary work of hometown heroes.

I no longer use the term because it is just too triggering. I've realized that the more effective and important idea is *show* what we mean rather than tell. A little controversy to catch people's attention is good, but we want to avoid needless strife that sows confusion and bad will.

Now don't get it twisted. I'm not saying that everybody is going to love you just because you don't use triggering phrases. If you are working to make a change anywhere, haters gonna hate sometimes.

Creating a New Future

The institutionalization of systemic racism is foundational to capitalism in America. That aspect of White supremacy created windfalls of legal profiteering for White Americans as it denied Blacks and other communities of color similar generational wealth accumulation benefits. This has extended the duration of second-class status initiated under slavery such that today, we use terms like "low income," "Black," and "Latino" interchangeably.

In low-status communities, "low income" is often associated with neighborhood preservation by the nonprofit industrial complex. In effect, the mixing of these terms serves to equate poverty with culture—a huge mistake and a feature of American society that is self-reinforcing and very difficult to change.

Just like in every other community, ambitious, talented people are born in low-status communities. Our research indicates that people in low-status communities have hopes, dreams, and aspirations for their lives. Unfortunately, many people feel they can experience these hopes, dreams, and aspirations only outside of their community—they were led to believe that success is measured by how far away they are able to get from their community.

If you were to look at who is participating in real estate development in low-status communities, you would find that overwhelmingly it is not the people who are born and raised there.

Although racial disparities do exist in education and opportunity, and these factors diminish the chances that individuals will experience success, they don't eliminate successes. The Cinderella story of rags to riches does happen, and it's a happy story that we should celebrate! But why is there no expectation or even encouragement that some of the successful people engage *directly* in the redevelopment of their own communities?

I'd like to help establish an alternative narrative regarding who gets to redevelop low-status communities and what that development could look like. Our approach might be considered problematic by some, and sometimes, it does feel lonely when I stick my neck out. However, I remain encouraged because I know I am not alone. I am not the only one getting caught trying to accomplish what the late congressman John Lewis famously called "good trouble," and I'd like to share the work of three of my favorite fellow troublemakers.

East Bay Permanent Real Estate Cooperative: Urging Divestment from Wall Street to Oakland's Seventh Street

I was attending a summit hosted by the US Green Building Council that focused on equity within the built environment movement when I first heard of the work of the East Bay Permanent Real Estate Cooperative (EBPREC). The group planned to buy a property in Oakland collectively and use it as a vehicle to support permanent, affordable mixed-use space for the benefit of their resident owners.

I immediately became EBPREC's East Coast fangirl. (Please note, I mean "fan" in the traditional sense, not euphemistically, as I describe my most ardent detractors.) Even though they were three thousand miles away, I signed myself up to participate in EBPREC's lunchtime learning sessions, which they offered to the local community to help people better understand various aspects of real estate investment and development.

EBPREC is led by the inimitable third-generation West Oaklander Noni Session and an amazingly talented team, who are well versed in community outreach, finance, and real estate. They use a traditional, market-based real estate investment strategy (debt and equity), donated land, public and private partnerships, and city funds and incentives when available coupled with an ethos based on supporting local residents.

What excited me most about their process was the portion of the equity from crowdfunded cash investments by local community members. Most important is their concept of derisking investments on behalf of their community members. Get this: *there is no buy-in cost to become a resident owner in EBPREC.* Folks are brought in to resident ownership strictly on the basis of their value as humans.

Their investors were a multiracial group of people with a credo that openly acknowledged the legacy of systemic racism and how it historically discriminated against wealth creation possibilities for Black, Latino, and Indigenous people. They all agreed to participate in a process that centered its efforts on demonstrably benefiting the people for whom the ability to pursue the American Dream has been denied.

EBPREC's first three projects created twelve units of permanent, affordable housing that are owned, occupied, and operated by members of the collective. Participants were actively engaged in every aspect of the process, including identifying properties, acquisition, design, visioning, financing, and even construction.

This type of collective ownership pays a real financial and equally real and valuable spiritual return on investment to everyone involved. This is in stark contradistinction to how affordable housing is created and managed currently, wherein large blocks of outside capital are able to unlock access to government subsidies that are unattainable by, for example, an individual property owner who might want to provide affordability through their rental units.

The developers in control of outside capitals coupled with the support of government subsidies, build a project in an area they will likely not live in or near or will not be affected positively or negatively by the long-term outcomes of their decisions. Those developers are legally within their rights to function as they do, and not all of what they do is bad, but without helping to turn the tide of racial disparity in American wealth creation, I would argue that none of it is truly great.

I find it galling how the philanthropic sector has systematically avoided using its vast capital reserves to enable wealth creation in the real estate development of low-status communities. And its ironic given that many of the major foundations built their endowments on real estate development profits—on top of a legacy of racial exclusion in that very sector. As the saying goes, "History doesn't repeat itself, but it rhymes."

EBPREC is currently developing a $4.8 million mixed-use project called Esther's Orbit Room & Cultural Arts Center that pays homage to Oakland's rich cultural arts history. Legendary artists such as B. B. King, Prince, MC Hammer, and the Rolling Stones all credit Seventh Street for a portion of their commercial and critical success. That history will provide a fitting backdrop for Black artists, makers, and creators in almost seven thousand square feet of commercial space and permanent affordable housing for seven to ten artists.

EBPREC has also formed strategic partnerships with foundations that are not just offering platitudes of support like so many within the nonprofit industrial complex. Instead, they are lending significant capital to EBPREC's financing. A notable player is the Kataly Foundation, led by Nwamaka Agbo, the creator of a restorative economics framework that provides an alternative model for philanthropy to follow in support of community-led wealth-building initiatives.

Oaklanders will be able to enjoy a walkable Black cultural corridor that includes a cafe and juice bar, fine art gallery, performance venue, farmers market, and classroom space, as well as a community healing space. It's the kind of place that Oaklanders have dreamed of for a while and now they are manifesting it! Not coincidentally, these same pieces of lifestyle infrastructure were also reflected in our surveys here in the South Bronx.

Community Action and Planning Group: A Mother's Pain Becomes Fuel for Regeneration

Reflecting on losing her son to gun violence in Toronto, Canada, Symone Walters made this statement to CBS News in September 2013: "Why must we leave our neighborhood where we grew up just so we can be safe and our children free from harm? We have to make changes here—so that families and children have access to opportunities and don't live in fear."[2]

Not a far cry from the subtitle of this book. I hear her loud and clear. In my years wrestling with the herd of crazy forces hurled against us, I have been at my best looking past the "end of fear" phase of community development, and what a great future would look like, in my opinion. I am always happy to hear and discuss other opinions and ideas too.

We can agree that it is far too common to hear about young lives lost to gun violence in America. Although the United States does has the highest rates of gun-related deaths in a country that is technically a nonconflict zone,[3] other countries are not exempt, including our otherwise peaceful neighbor to the north.

In the Jane-Finch neighborhood of Toronto, Canada, fifteen-year-old Tahj Loor Walters was riding his bicycle to a nearby shopping center when he was shot by two men in a vehicle before they fled the scene. Tahj died in a hospital two weeks later.

The Black folks who immigrated to Toronto from the Caribbean and First Nations people are clustered in crowded housing projects, with poor schools and few legitimate economic opportunities. Tahj was a victim of a conflict between rival gangs, which, in turn, was a result of the lack of social and economic infrastructure in the community.

Soon after losing Tahj, Symone sat with another mother who had recently lost a son to gun violence. She didn't want anyone else to go through the agony they were experiencing and would every day for the rest of their lives. So she joined a community group active in Jane-Finch, the Community Action and Planning Group, and focused on assessing the conditions that led her son—and others—to this type of death, which she saw as a byproduct of a community that failed to live up to its own potential.

The architecture of the community was bleak: towering housing projects with attached public spaces designed and maintained using the least effort and expense. There were few parks or other spaces for the community to gather for active or passive recreation, and all of these were visually unappealing. There were few gathering spots for neighbors to get together for activities that fostered a shared sense of community such as sports or art projects. However, drug activity flourished openly.

Within the buildings themselves, "community center" space was provided, but you would not hang out there, nor do striving and successful residents in this community. Without dedicated support for programming or viable day-to-day commercial activity, those areas were most often vacant.

Instead of trying to repurpose an overall architecture of passive oppression and low expectations, Symone was drawn to transforming nearby vacant land owned by the Metrolinx commuter railway. Metrolinx initially had planned to sell the land after it was done using it to stage construction equipment and supplies.

Symone imagined that this barren area, long visible to the community, could be transformed into economic activity with the Finch West Light Rail Transit connected future.

Canada is spending $2.5 billion on this transportation infrastructure project.[4] As the Jane-Finch community becomes linked to other parts of Toronto, more economic prospects will emerge. It's important to attach these developments to community goals and aspirations in strategic ways and not to create just another "youth organization" or community center. Are we creatively preparing for the young adults who emerge from the youth organizations to access the fruits of the new urban development projects?

Armed with only an unwavering commitment to make her community better, Symone dived into planning. She and the Community Action and Planning Group connected with Rosemarie Powell of the Toronto Community Benefits Network, a leading community-labor coalition with experience negotiating among larger infrastructure agencies and corporations. Symone needed them on the team and leveraged their assets, which saved her own energy and bandwidth for other challenges to come. Together, they collaborated to negotiate and secure a Community Benefits Agreement (CBA) with Metrolinx.

A CBA is a contract between a community and a company or agency seeking to locate operations there. Elected officials are not part of the agreement because of perceived or real conflicts of interest.

The Jane-Finch CBA boasts both a land transfer and a concerted union job creation effort for local residents.[5] A key provision is two acres of land for a sixty-five thousand-square-foot activity hub in this long neglected community. Everything in the hub will be dedicated to spaces and programs that support a nourishing environment for the local economic, artistic, and human development of Jane-Finch.

The vision of Symone and her partners includes animating the streetscape with small-scale retail commercial rentals, including a multipurpose theatre/gym, a community-run cafe, and an art gallery space. They also are in the process of developing youth-specific content with the community. Within two years of the start of the project, thirty-one construction jobs were created for Black and other youth of color via apprenticeship programs, and sixteen professional, technical, and administrative jobs and more employment opportunities are coming on line as the project progresses.[6]

I have personal experience introducing a project that could have transformed a community and then being summarily dismissed by government agencies and development companies to do as they saw fit. So a part of me cringed at hearing Symone's big, bold vision—I don't want to see the same thing happen to her! Symone and the community can easily get swept to the side when players at this scale come together.

But Symone and her partners are doing everything they can to stay at the table. It's not always possible for one person on the community side to sustain the effort needed to stay in the game throughout the deal. So she has inculcated a multigenerational group of local individuals at different points in their lives to offset the amount of time each individual is required to spend to keep the CBA on track. The Community Action and Planning Group is still part of the CBA process. Additionally, Symone's close relationship with the Toronto Community Benefits Network helps ensure that they have the heft of the powerful community-labor coalition alongside them.

They are building *institutional power* and are not depending on the strength of any one individual. Symone (or others in her place) could fall into a role that no person can easily fulfill alone. She has found, and continues to find, new and strategic allies to help realize the community's goals.

The next challenge is the "capital stack." Whether you are in the nonprofit sector, have a franchise, or are involved in real estate development at any level, when you want to put a building on the ground and your money is coming from several sources, it's helpful to look at it like a stack of cash, with different amounts coming from different contributors, such as bank loans, grants, cash reserves, future revenue, and equity partners. Symone is putting her George Brown College education to work, where her social work degree required that she present a solution to a social problem with a solid business plan.

Symone saw the land as a viable path to wellness that her community had not experienced since the ancestors of her First Nations neighbors lived on these lands. She is now living out her commitment through this land transfer, which will allow her to manifest her determination to keep other families from suffering the way she did.

Jumpstart Germantown: Philanthropy Not Required (but Welcomed)

Several years ago, I read an article about a project in Philadelphia called Jumpstart Philly that was getting aspiring developers, mostly women and people of color, into the real estate industry. I was dumbfounded by its laser focus on creating value for the people and communities involved in its programs, yet it had no parallel in New York City—none whatsoever. I considered trying to start a chapter in the South Bronx, but then I slipped into the never-ending river of work, tasks, pursuits, information, and everything else competing for my attention and I sort of forgot about it.

Years later, I was awarded an Edmund N. Bacon Urban Design Award in Philadelphia, and as part of the day's festivities, I was invited to a lunch at the site of the founding chapter, Jumpstart Germantown. I was so impressed at seeing and hearing the successful participants as we went around the table during introductions.

Nobody talked about community land trusts, affordable rental housing, or what government and developers "should" do. Those assembled were predominantly Black folks, mostly from the hood, talking about construction-to-permanent loans, price per square foot, debt-to-equity ratios to finance their next project, and partnering with other Jumpstart alumni on acquisition financing with defined exit criteria and payout schedules.

I may have been the guest of honor since I was getting the award, but clearly these folks knew more than I did and were executing on a path that was replacing chronic blight with an improved local quality of life and healthy profits that enabled their next projects to proceed apace.

It was a system that expanded virally with each new graduate lighting the way for new cohorts. All Jumpstarters were supplied with the first couple of real estate loans they needed to succeed, unlike the statistically racist US banking system, well known to deny Black developers working in low-status communities. These were not finite grants with arbitrary qualifications and prescribed not-for-profit uses. These were starter loans that paved the way to much larger traditional capital resources.

The projects were not just offering more affordable rentals but allowed ownership. They could include a place for a single home-owner to live in or multiple properties rented or sold to others who lived alongside the developers in the communities where they grew up.

The basis was not a profit and tax subsidy export model but real local capital circulation with the ability to attract more outside capital into the hands of local developers.

I asked when the next cohort was to begin. The answer was "tomorrow."

Without hesitation, I cleared my calendar. Vashti Du Bois, a fel-low Wesleyan alum and Philly transplant who transformed part of her beautiful Germantown home into the Colored Girls Museum, which "honors the stories, experiences, and history of ordinary Col-ored Girls" like me,[7] offered to let me crash at her place so that I could experience this phenomenon firsthand. For the next four Wednes-days, I was on the BoltBus to Philly!

Jumpstart Germantown (and now Jumpstart Philly) is a unique community development program in Philadelphia that loans private capital resources directly to real estate projects and provides rigor-ous training so residents become the tools for their own economic empowerment, redeveloping the community from the inside out. The founder, Ken Weinstein, is a New Jersey–born commercial real estate developer with over thirty years of experience developing formerly vacant, deteriorated properties in his adopted hometown of Philadel-phia. He always seemed warm, approachable, and quick to smile with some Bruce Springsteen swagger.

Jumpstart Germantown began when Ken was at a local commu-nity meeting for one of his projects and, as he recalls, the meeting did not go well for him (I know that feeling). He was grilled hard about every detail and was worried that his project would not gain approval.

One young Black man and one young White woman in attendance watched him go through the process of defending his project. At the end of the meeting, they approached him, commiserated, and asked his advice on how they could follow his example to restore blighted residential properties in their own community. Germantown is a predominantly Black neighborhood in Philadelphia that has a great deal of vacant and blighted properties amid an incredible variety of architectural beauty.

Ken offered to spend a few hours with them at his office to give them the basics of real estate development. As a commercial developer, he was excited that these young people wanted to focus on residential development where he began his career. Ken understood that improving those blighted properties would increase the value of his commercial developments nearby, while his commercial developments would simultaneously add value to their residential properties. It was a win-win for all involved!

Those two young people told their friends, who told more of their friends, about this cool White guy who was willing to share what seemed like impenetrable industry secrets. Ken found himself acting as an informal and very busy trainer, networker, lender, and mentor.

Although he thoroughly enjoyed teaching, it was an unsustainable dynamic. He didn't want to neglect his own work or stop the flow of Philly's newest developers. He launched Jumpstart Germantown as a codified sixteen-hour program led by him and recruited his colleagues, all leaders in the Philly real estate, finance, and city government communities, to serve as guest instructors.

Ken didn't stop there.

Most new developers did not qualify for a bank loan for their first few projects since they did not have a track record. In addition, bank lending is not immune to racial bias. In fact, several anecdotes have emerged recently that show how even third-party property value appraisals, which are used to determine refinancing amounts, change when evidence of Black ownership is kept from the appraisers.

Ken personally financed a $5 million revolving loan fund that offered first loans to brand-new developers who completed the Jumpstart training—assuming they could legitimately demonstrate on paper how their project was going to be solvent.

So far, more than fifteen hundred folks have graduated from the Jumpstart Training Program, which now includes eight local chapters in Philadelphia; Norristown, Pennsylvania; and Wilmington, Delaware. To date, more than $30 million has been financed through the loan program with a 0 percent default rate. Many times that amount was brought into Philly's economy because new developers were given an opportunity to grow by one guy who was open to a fair market exchange of value, hard work, and vision—an island in a sea of the nonprofit industrial complex's low expectations and paternalism and the federally guaranteed banking industry's unreformed racial bias.

And the two intrepid young people who first approached Ken, Bruce McCall and Nancy Deephouse, are now leaders among Philly's successful next generation of local real estate developers and have gone on to produce dozens of successful buy-and-holds and fix-and-flips.

What Do These Examples Say about Us?

These are only a few of my favorite examples that inspire me to believe that we can step away from status quo development that maintains perpetual victimhood within low-status communities.

The activist community, though arguably well-intended, and opportunistic real estate and financial players are locked in a symbiotic relationship that keeps the same wheel turning, despite perfunctory public grumbling on both sides, and an ever widening wealth gap between White people and everyone else. However, as all of these examples have shown, we can redirect the talent and passion of people with sensitivity to socioeconomic inequality in America away from the typical trap of perpetuating the nonprofit-government cycle or taking away low-status communities' talent to improve and build up other communities.

Money-making ventures that produce positive and locally felt benefits for the community are possible. They are elusive changes, desired but unattained—a half century after the victories of a historic civil rights movement.

Another factor undermining beneficial community revitalization is that the jobs that focus on social fixes within nonprofit and government sector monopolies are not attractive, from a salary or lifestyle standpoint, to many of the talented young adults from low-status communities who would be most sensitive to the larger situation. Thus the talent best qualified to turn around capital flows (generated by both economic stagnation and displacement) are diverted from using their talents within their own communities.

Not only does the compensation compare poorly to what they can make elsewhere, these individuals also face a wall of resistance to dispersing market power to those who have been historically excluded. Nonprofit boards, philanthropy organizations, government policies, and those who work within the involved agencies historically have been known to execute policies that frown on Black ambition. Pop stars and athletes are acceptable—perhaps because they number in the low thousands at any given time and provide a bright, shiny distraction from the very, very large amounts of capital moving under the surface and away from predominantly Black and Latino American citizens.

The solutions discussed above may be considered controversial by some because they openly embrace the tools of capitalism without doctrine or quixotic ideals meant to replace capitalism. But they offer an alternative and viable approach to community development that centers the local community as the direct financial beneficiary.

Or, to paraphrase Snoop Dogg, you want to keep your mind on your money and your money on your mind because if you don't, someone else will.

CHAPTER 19

IDEA TO REALITY =
DISCIPLINE + WORK + TIME

I know you have plenty of other things to do, so I appreciate that you are reading this far or even just skimming this book. And I hope I am not being presumptuous to believe that if you are reading this, it's because you are (or want to be) involved in some sort of change around you, and you want to ensure that your work matters.

I know how you feel. I want my life to be useful. I want to make the dreams for my community, and communities like them, real.

If I had had the ability to look into my future twenty-some years ago and I had seen that this girl from the ghetto would become a leader in urban revitalization strategy through project-based development and policy leadership, I would have asked my future self, "Wait. What exactly are you doing?" I don't necessarily have an answer on any given day. Yet here I am.

Oftentimes, when I present my work publicly, folks will say, "I'm just an average person. How can I do anything like *that?*"

My close friends and family will tell you just how average I am (with lots of love, mind you), but my happy truth is, I am a very average person, fearfully and wonderfully made, just like everybody else. Everyone, everywhere you look, has untapped capacity to create something awesome around them.

I believe what folks *really* need are insights regarding an approach to their challenges that attracts the right combination of forces—to get the job done. That's my secret sauce.

I am that girl from the ghetto who is still evolving as a practitioner, and my path was not smooth or linear. I learned hard lessons along the way. One that I want to share now is meant to help people break through the bottlenecks experienced at all levels, on ideas big or small—especially where the champion of an idea is not in a position to unilaterally make it happen, which is most of the time.

Whether we are talking about enacting government policies, shifting family dynamics, starting a business, or creating changes within a large or small corporation or government agency, getting the right people aligned with your idea is the single biggest challenge. Once you have buy-in at strategic points along your development timeline, money, land, creative interpretation of rules and regulations, favors, and all sorts of other pieces start falling into place.

Change—whether it's related to consumer purchasing habits; sexism, racism, or any other ism; or just a better (but potentially disruptive) approach to doing things—is always met with the human inertia to resist change. Rejection has nothing to do with the quality of your vision; it's natural. How you get through, around, over, or under the rejection is up to you and your willingness to adapt your vision. Remember, you're a human too—and you resist change just like everyone else does. Don't fall so much in love with your idea that you can't accept its changing along the way. There's about a 100 percent chance that it will change in some way.

Ready to Make Some Moves?

As America's demographic ratios change, new challenges and opportunities in sectors as seemingly disparate as conservation, technology, and public health are all evolving. We can view these changes as assets that can encourage everyone to contribute their very best. Even if we are not the change agents per se, we can help support change in many smaller ways once we recognize the dynamic underway.

Social entrepreneurs, real estate developers, economic development professionals, business and nonprofit leaders, midlevel corporate team members, startup entrepreneurs, and others who are structuring new types of professional relationships all have something to gain— and contribute! That is efficient and rewarding because it leverages all kinds of diverse resources that drive innovation.

Getting you, or you and your team, your resources, and your vision past the bottlenecks depends on executing leadership that encourages and builds on diverse opinions and perspectives—ultimately leading to effective action.

Elizabeth Streb, the MacArthur-winning dancer-choreographer-daredevil said it well: "Anything that's too safe is not action."[1] I never said it would always be comfortable, but do you want to live with the regret of always being safe?

Building a Better Toaster

The filter I put up to all my ideas for projects to determine whether or not I proceed can be humbling. It dismisses all sanctimony, self-perceived entitlement, and the notion of what others "should" do. You have to acknowledge and respect where you are in relation to the market or audience that you need.

The indicators along the way can inform your pivots—but if you're not careful, you'll hit a dead end that you could have seen coming. Your final outcome may look very different from what you originally envisioned if you remain attuned to what people are telling you both directly and between the lines.

You start by thinking about your idea as if you are selling a simple product, like a new and improved toaster, for example, and you need to get to a product launch. So imagine your idea, and pretend that concept is a toaster.

Whether your interest is in government policy, a company's organizational procedures, bringing a product or service to market, or promoting your own leadership within any organization that includes other humans—a reductive perspective helps place you and the project on a development timeline, with benchmarks you'll need to establish before moving on to the next step.

It's the strategy I have been using all this time and I enjoy sharing it with other doers. It requires discipline, work, and time. Great things will not come to you unless you are active about creating a different outcome. Any project will require a plan to move it from a self-indulgent *idea* to more widely accepted *reality*.

Here are the steps:

1. *Identify a market need.* What problem is out there that folks want solved *and* you are passionate about solving? Be honest and *stop* here if nobody is experiencing that need or if it is already filled by somebody else.

2. *Design an attractive solution.* What's your big idea? Is it something that has been tried before? Is your solution different? Better? Necessary? How will it be better than what is currently available?

3. *Find an angel investor or supporter.* The support you need could be money. It could be a person or a group of influencers who anoint your solution worthy of further attention. It might be a network that the right person introduces you to. Or it might be an organization already doing something similar or complementary that you can partner with.

4. *Launch a beta test.* You have to *show* something different. Talk is cheap—and sometimes annoying. Get something out there to demonstrate that at least one aspect of your solution is meeting the market need you have identified.

5. *Learn and refine (based on real-world reaction to your beta test).* Don't just admire the fruits of your labor. See how people use, don't use, or abuse your solution and *pay attention* to what

their actions and reactions tell you so you can adjust your perspective on design, audience, or market. You might design a solution for one purpose or group of users, and it gets adopted by a different group for different purposes than you imagined. Is this still a win? Be open to what they are teaching you.

6. *Reiterate and expand.* How the real world treats a small portion of your idea will tell you how best to modify the design to garner greater market acceptance, attract more powerful allies, borrow cash, sell equity, or possibly drop the whole thing and move on to something else.

You are a creative person who will have many ideas over your lifetime. Don't get hung up on one of them that nobody else cares about—to the exclusion of all the other great stuff you are capable of—unless you are convinced that you are right and have done the work to back it up.

Take, for example, Dune Lankard, a proud member of the Eyak Native Athabaskan tribe in Alaska. He offers a great example of an idea that went from fierce resistance to the building block of an even more ambitious plan.

No Good Deed Goes Unpunished, but Sometimes It Pays Off

Let's view Dune's impressive body of work through an idea-to-reality framework.

Market Need According to Dune

Dune identified a need to protect the local culture and environment while enabling the tribes to make money.

Dune was a commercial fisherman when he was approached by biologists and non-Native fishermen to consider organizing the tribes to accept restoration settlement funds from the 1989 *Exxon*

Valdez oil spill. Their proposal was to purchase and retire development rights of some of the nearly 44 million acres of land held by Indigenous Alaskans as part of the Alaska Native Claims Settlement Act (ANCSA).[2]

Dune's Attractive Solution

Dune's solution centered on land conservation that enabled long-term sustainable economic activity settlement funds to come to the Alaskan tribes. In this way, the tribes would be able to invest the proceeds as they chose and the land would be saved in perpetuity for hunting, fishing, tourism, and subsistence. However, because of environmental impacts, harmful clear-cut logging operations would be eliminated.

When Dune proposed the idea of conservation to his fellow members of the board of the Eyak Corporation, which managed the tribe's land rights, he was quickly labeled one of the "most hated men" among many of his fellow Indigenous people for championing an environmental policy that his peers felt would diminish their tribe's ability to make a living from logging.

In exchange for his advocacy to protect the environment as well as the culture of the land that supported fishing and their Native people for eons, Dune was verbally abused, physically threatened, unceremoniously kicked off the board of the Eyak Corporation, and sued for standing up for the land and his people. He had a fan club of his very own.

Finding Angel Investors and Supporters

In his search for support, Dune realized that prophets are rarely appreciated in their own hometowns.

Dune was undaunted in his efforts to share the validity of his idea. As you look for your own "angels," be aware that you won't often have a parade of people pulling out all the stops to support you. You just might have, like Dune had, a strong and pivotal minority: some other tribes were receptive to the idea and supported his advocacy.

Launching a Beta Test

Those initial efforts paid off. By 1998, Dune's efforts resulted in a $380 million fund for Native Alaskan corporations, protecting over seven hundred thousand acres of coastal habitat, which enriched a dozen or so Native Alaskan corporations and thousands of ANCSA shareholders (tribal members).

Learn and Refine, Based on Real-World Reaction to Your Beta

The project grew to encompass more land and more money, but the local culture was preserved.

Since then, Dune has gone on to preserve another three hundred thousand acres of wild salmon habitat and after twenty-seven years helped extend the political *Exxon Valdez* Oil Spill restoration boundary to include his beloved Copper River Delta in its entirety, which will lead to more preservation of endangered wildlife and wild salmon habitat.

Reiterating and Expanding

Today, Dune's attention is still in coastal areas, but this time it's underwater—in kelp and mariculture (bivalve) farming.

Kelp can sequester up to 20 percent more carbon from the air than land-based forests and grows eighteen to twenty-four inches per day, making it an important component in the fight against climate change. It is a traditional food source, and kelp has a unique ability to be transformed into a multitude of products—from beauty products to food products and even pharmaceuticals. Bivalves (e.g., scallops, mussels, clams, and oysters) can filter forty to sixty gallons of water each per day.

Dune's concern now is that the big multinational (and international) seafood processors are already lining up to privatize the oceans for corporate gain by permitting their own kelp and mariculture farming operations, which would limit Native sovereignty and tribal rights to food security.

Because of the detrimental impacts of climate change (e.g., ocean acidification, warming of the oceans, and ocean rise) Dune is offering a more restorative approach—for the ocean, for the land, and for the people. His plan is to raise capital for an innovative food system and advanced wave energy freezer technology for over thirty interested Alaskan tribes. The freezing system would give each of the tribes the ability to efficiently flash freeze seafoods, wild game, and vegetables, including kelp and mariculture species harvested from the sea, so that traditional food sources can be preserved in a higher quality state for longer periods of time and with minimum freezer burn and they run on renewable energy. With climate change, food preservation issues are paramount to Native peoples since Alaska's permafrost, sea ice, and glaciers are melting at unprecedented rates.

He has already garnered a great deal of attention and is making great strides toward building a restorative-based economy throughout his cherished ancestral homelands. This type of development is meant to give younger, striving members of Dune's and neighboring tribes an ongoing and expanding incentive to see their future in Alaska—and not go south to the big cities to find their fortune. That more typical generational path out the door undermines all other social metrics and makes it easier for better organized and well-funded corporations and government agencies to call the shots—often at the long-term expense of the people and the environment.

Dune does operate with a cultural and moral code regarding harmony with nature. He loves nature, and he recognizes its value to different constituencies that look at the habitat of his 5.5 million acre

Chugach National Forest and 17 million acre Copper River Delta "neighborhood."

He might not win any popularity contests, at least not in the short term, but he's forging a path with restorative commercial real estate development that others will run with and grow long after he leaves this earth. And that's what we are talking about here: creating generational patterns of wealth-building potential that stretch greater and greater with each passing decade and, in these climate changing times, each passing day.

When another financial crisis happens—and it will—no matter how bad it is, the banks will most likely come out okay. But massive numbers of individuals will lose what they had or see their goals grow further and further out of their reach—unless the right infrastructure is put in place.

It's not the easy way for sure, but being prepared to turn to weather the storm, requires thinking and acting like Dune has—for the benefit of all.

Where Do You Fit In?

Comparing your world-changing brilliant idea to a toaster is not meant to diminish you or your vision in any way, but it is a good way to think about the rigor you need to apply to your vision so that it can live outside your head.

I have not devoted my time to launching a new kind of toaster because I use one that looks like the one I grew up with in the 1970s, and it works pretty well as far as I can tell. But let's say you are passionate about toast. Could there be a better way to produce toasted bread in the home? The answer is almost certainly yes.

If you were passionate about this topic, I bet you would make sure that at least some other people were dissatisfied by the current results of their home toasting method. That's where the discipline comes in.

You might come up with a design that improves the situation, appeal to some type of angel investor appropriate to this market space, and launch a beta version to observe how average consumers react before going big into the world toaster domination market. Along the way you learn so much by listening, observing, asking the same question three different ways, and meeting the right person who leads you to another person who teaches you something else about toast.

Now if you have enough imagination to walk yourself through the intricacies of the toaster market, imagine what you can do when you apply yourself to coming up with ideas that make your community the place you dream about.

In other words:

Get. Caught. Trying.

You'll thank me later.

EPILOGUE

Many months after the cafe opened, I was coming back uptown after some meetings in Manhattan. I came out of the Hunts Point Avenue subway station, and on my way home, I ran into a young man who frequented the cafe.

We walked in the same direction further into the neighborhood, making small talk. He shared how much he liked having something as nice as the cafe in the neighborhood.

After walking about a block, he asked, "Where are you going? Isn't the cafe closed now?"

"Yeah, it's closed. I'm on my way home."

He stopped dead in his tracks.

"*You? Live here?*"

I had heard similar sentiments from others before like

- "You made it out, but you still give back!"
- "It's so nice that you haven't forgotten about your old neighborhood. You know, we really appreciate you."
- "Majora, I am so proud of you and what you do for our community! So where do you live now?"

Of course I take great delight in the fact that many folks appreciate the fruits of my labor. When it happens, and it often does, I consider them love notes from God.

But the young man and others who are genuinely surprised that I still live in the neighborhood confirm that there is a pervasive attitude in low-status communities all over the world: successful people don't stay in our communities.

Their comments make my heart hurt because whenever it happens, I am revisited by the bitter shame I once felt by my association with a place considered a national symbol of urban blight. I felt that we were viewed as only problems to be solved.

Loving your neighbors as much as you love yourself is the second most important tenet of my Christian faith, following only behind loving God with all your passion and prayer and intelligence and energy.[1] My work is the manifestation of my love for my hometown and others like it.

So when I hear comments from people like the ones I mentioned, I see myself fully in their eyes:

- Recognized for working hard and loving up on my community
- Appreciated for the efforts but not considered a part of it anymore

Their words are an invitation for me to share how much I want more of us to enjoy beautiful things in our own communities with friends, family, and neighbors. Why do we always have to go to somebody else's neighborhood to do so? I want to stem the outflow of our best and brightest so that we can luxuriate in our own self-created shine.

I watch their eyes as they think about it, contemplating something they never even considered before. And then to a person, they take a breath and say something to the effect of "Yeah, we *should* have more of that."

More of That

I've spent the last nineteen chapters sharing my thoughts on why folks might feel as though they have to move out of their neighborhoods to live in better ones and how we can counteract that notion by helping our neighbors understand that they are the keys to our own recovery.

My greatest hope is that more of us from low-status communities see the value of giving our own hometowns a second look. We can make them into the communities of our dreams. I want to shed some light and love on them so that people can see the beauty of themselves and others reflected in their neighborhoods.

I also hope that those in positions of power and authority might recognize themselves somewhere in the pages of this book and find inspiration and courage to do something different. Treating low-status communities as odd collections of second-class citizens, patronized wards of the state, or cash cows is an easy trap to fall into, even by well-intentioned folks.

I know that if even a few of us work together strategically, the lives of people in low-status communities will change for the better. We will create more places where joy and happiness can grow.

Once upon a time, I did believe that people like me, born in places like the one I lived in, were deficient somehow and that my best hope was to get as far away from there as I could. Perhaps embedded in my neural pathways, passed down through generations of enslavement and discrimination, is the history of Black folks in America, leading me to believe that escape was my best option.

I once defined myself as an expression of the blight that others deemed my community to be. Now I can look directly at the shame that I had felt because of who I am and where I am from. I know now that the only power it had over me was what I gave it.

I am still that little girl who sat on her father's lap to share plans for the house she wanted to live in, the same kid who wanted her parents and her neighbors to be proud of her, the same wet-behind-the-ears developer who became comfortable with being uncomfortable because she embraced her own ambition and power, even though it was denied by some.

No one will ever make me want to run away again. I will continue to use my talents toward helping low-status communities everywhere to remind them that they can do the same.

By demonstrating that we do not have to participate in a cycle that adds to our collective failures, we can show that building landscapes of hope and possibility are achievable in places that have been written off all across America and in our hearts.

No one should have to move out of their neighborhood to live in a better one.

RECLAIMING YOUR COMMUNITY
DISCUSSION GUIDE

I hope *Reclaiming Your Community* has opened up new questions about how real estate development and wealth creation in low-status communities are perceived and can be leveraged for positive change.

Some information and interpretations here may seem counterintuitive regarding subjects like poverty, gentrification, wealth, equality, social justice, and other terms. Reexamining long- and widely held assumptions about race, community, money, and so on is best done in conversation with other people to try to understand how we can stop repeating the same motions—despite not seeing meaningful improvements. That goes for our society, the whole world, or just what goes down on your block.

The questions below are divided into four groups (General, Families, Organizations, and Community Groups), but all of them are relevant for everybody! These questions are not meant to be asked or answered just once. Invite groups of people whom you frequently socialize with and those who might not always get together. Consider whipping out this discussion guide at your next family gathering, church picnic, class reunion, or fraternity, sorority, or Masonic event, as well as political activities. Who knows what you'll discover?

General

1. What do you think of the term "low-status community" versus more commonly used terms like "low income," "deprived," "underprivileged," and so on?
2. Why is affordable housing most often assumed to be rented and not owned?
3. How has access to favorable financing and capital been denied to Black home buyers up until and including today?
4. How is it possible for low-status communities to turn around economically without racial displacement, and if racial displacement doesn't happen, would the turnaround still be considered gentrification?
5. In what ways is poverty considered a cultural attribute?
6. Is a talent-retention approach to neighborhood revitalization realistic in your opinion? Why? Why not?
7. What do you believe is the root cause of so-called gentrification and how are urban population increases related to displacement?

Families

1. How are assets that are held by any of your elderly family members part of a clear succession plan—with easy-to-understand options demonstrating the pros and cons of different inheritance and investment scenarios?
2. How do you feel about unleveraged value in homes or property owned by members of your close or extended family that could be leveraged for purposes you can all agree on, such as college or training tuitions, additional property purchases, consolidation of higher interest debts, and so on, without liquidating those assets?
3. Are you taking collective steps and sharing information to improve credit scores among members of your friends and family network? Explain.
4. Where and how have you sought out financial literacy about a topic that was challenging and presented you with new or

confusing information? Have you shared this experience with others?

5. What do you believe needs to happen for Black Wall Streets to exist again in America?

Organizations

1. How does your company, nonprofit, or government agency use strategies for reducing brain drain in communities you are focused on or operate in?

2. What are some talent-retention strategies that would make your organization or community more attractive to people who have options to go elsewhere?

3. What can be done to help young adults on their way up see potential in your neighborhood or community of interest that your organization could support?

4. Is there organizational capacity where you are (or at connected organizations) to intervene in the liquidation of property held by or to be acquired by people of color? How can you help keep more land from slipping out of community member control?

5. How are infrastructure investments in local mass transit, parks, greenways, or restored waterways viewed as indicators of future real estate appreciation opportunities? How are property owners of color in those areas helped to secure their assets and the wealth-building potential that accompanies government infrastructure investment?

6. How is maintaining existing low-income homeownership an important goal in terms of cost-effective affordable housing in your city?

Community Groups

1. What are neighbors willing to share about their financial situation with regard to property ownership, debt, and so on? Start by offering up what you feel comfortable with and go from there.

2. Are there types of businesses outside your community where you frequently spend money?
   a. Would you like to see something similar nearby?
   b. What would it take to achieve that?
3. What commonly recurring challenges to your community's quality of life (e.g., dog poo, loud/late music, garbage, pests) can you approach local government to help solve?
4. Is poverty a defining attribute of your community or local culture? If so, why do you think that is so?
5. When a community member is more financially successful than their peers, do they become culturally less authentic in your opinion? Why or why not?
6. Who are some of the local individuals leading on aspects of community reinvestment and wealth creation currently where you live? Do they have your support? Why or why not? Are you one of them?

NOTES

Preface

1. Juan Gonzalez, "Public School 48 in the Bronx Discovers Slave Burial Ground in Nearby Joseph Rodman Drake Park," *New York Daily News*, May 23, 2013.

Introduction

1. Denard Cummings (MPA, director, Equitable Health System Integration) in discussion with the author, June 4, 2021.

2. Elizabeth Sperber, Ozge Sensoy Bahar, and Fred M. Ssewamala, "Implications of Race and Concentrated Poverty for Asset Development Policy: Evidence from an Exploratory Study in Harlem and the Bronx, New York," *Journal of Race and Policy* 13, no. 1 (Spring–Summer 2017): 20–40.

3. Elizabeth Kneebone and Natalie Holmes, "U.S. Concentrated Poverty in the Wake of the Great Recession," Brookings Institute, March 16, 2016, https://www.brookings.edu/research/u-s-concentrated-poverty-in-the-wake-of-the-great-recession/; and Emily Badger, "Black Poverty Differs from White Poverty," *Washington Post*, August 12, 2015, https://www.washingtonpost.com/news/wonk/wp/2015/08/12/black-poverty-differs-from-white-poverty/.

Chapter 2

1. Jonathan Mahler, *Ladies and Gentlemen, the Bronx Is Burning: 1977, Baseball, Politics, and the Battle for the Soul of a City* (New York: Farrar, Straus and Giroux, 2006).

Chapter 3

1. "Monocultures vs Biodiversity," Food, *TheLills.com*, 2018, https://thelills.com/monocultures-vs-biodiversity/.

2. Majora Carter Group, *Community Needs Assessment: Hunts Point Peninsula, Bronx*, HomeTOWN Security Laboratory, June 2013, https://drive.google.com/file/d/0B3z60xxEzFE2Y1E0VjVzbThyemc/.

3. Sharon Florentine, "Employee Retention: 8 Strategies for Retaining Top Talent," *CIO*, February 27, 2019, https://www.cio.com/article/2868419/how-to-improve-employee-retention.html.

4. Will Bredderman, "Politicians Air Grievances about Development Foes and Themselves," *Crain's New York Business*, June 6, 2018.

5. "Area Median Income," New York City Department of Housing Preservation and Development, accessed May 1, 2021, https://www1.nyc.gov/site/hpd/services-and-information/area-median-income.page.

Chapter 4

1. Sesali Bowen, "How *Scandal* Brought Black Twitter to Life Every Thursday," *Refinery 29*, April 19, 2018, https://www.refinery29.com/en-us/2018/04/196580/scandal-tv-show-black-twitter-history; and Neil Drumming, "'Scandal's' Racially Charged Motto: You Have to Be Twice as Good as Them," *Salon*, October 4, 2013.

Chapter 5

1. Liseli A. Fitzpatrick, "African Names and Naming Practices: The Impact Slavery and European Domination Had on the African Psyche, Identity and Protest" (master's thesis, Ohio State University, 2012), http://rave.ohiolink.edu/etdc/view?acc_num=osu1338404929.

2. Maurice Willows, *Disaster Relief Report Riot June 1921* (Tulsa, OH: Tulsa Historical Society and Museum, December 1921), https://www .tulsahistory.org/wp-content/uploads/2018/11/1921-Red-Cross-Report -December-30th.pdf; and Oklahoma Commission on Riot of 1921, *Tulsa Race Riot: A Report by the Oklahoma Commission to Study the Tulsa Race Riot of 1921* (CreateSpace Independent, 2001).

3. Kendrick Marshall, "'Signs of Gentrification': Greenwood Community Worries Residents Being Pushed Out, History Disrespected," *Tulsa World,* January 19, 2021.

4. Karen Duffin and Mary Childs, "Patent Racism," June 12, 2020, in *Planet Money,* NPR podcast.

5. Jay Farbstein, Emily Axelrod, Robert Shibley, and Richard Wener, *2009 Rudy Bruner Award Report: Silver Medal Winner: Hunts Point Riverside Park* (Cambridge, MA: Bruner Foundation, 2009).

Chapter 6

1. Ta-Nehisi Coates, "The Case for Reparations," *Atlantic,* June 2014, http://www.theatlantic.com/magazine/archive/2014/06/the-case-for -reparations/361631/.

2. Jung Hyun Choi, "Breaking Down the Black-White Homeownership Gap," *Urban Wire,* February 21, 2020, https://www.urban.org/urban-wire /breaking-down-black-white-homeownership-gap.

3. *AARP Livability Fact Sheet—Density,* AARP, 2014, https://www .aarp.org/livable-communities/info-2014/livability-factsheet-density.html. The Congress for the New Urbanism (cnu.org) defines *New Urbanism* as "a planning and development approach based on the principles of how cities and towns had been built for the last several centuries: walkable blocks and streets, housing and shopping in close proximity, and accessible public spaces. In other words: New Urbanism focuses on human-scaled urban design."

Chapter 8

1. Yi Zhou, "Studies on Poverty: A Controversy between the Theories of Structuralist Explanation and Cultural Explanation," Chinese Academy of Sciences, Beijing, 2002.

2. Joy Y. Coates, "Navigating Funding Access and Equity in the Philanthropic Ecosystem: A Narrative Study Exploring Leaders of Color Experiences Launching New Initiatives Amidst Disparities in Funding Opportunities through the Complexity Leadership Framework," (doctoral thesis, Northeastern University, 2020), https://repository.library. northeastern.edu/files/neu:m0472513f/fulltext.pdf; and Cheryl Dorsey et al., "Overcoming the Racial Bias in Philanthropic Funding," *Stanford Social Innovation Review*, May 4, 2020, https://ssir.org/articles/entry /overcoming_the_racial_bias_in_philanthropic_funding.

3. Isabel Allende, "Tales of Passion," filmed March 2007 at TED Conference, https://www.ted.com/talks/isabel_allende_tales_of_passion/transcript.

4. Ana Isabel Baptista and Adrienne Perovich, "Environmental Justice and Philanthropy: Challenges and Opportunities for Alignment—Gulf South and Midwest Case Studies," Tishman Environment and Design Center, 2020, https://static1.squarespace.com/static/5d14dab43967 cc000179f3d2/t/5e5e7781cccebf576948d365/1583249295033 /EJ+and+Philanthropy+Alignment+MW+and+GS_3.3.20_final.pdf.

Chapter 9

1. "Jimi Hendrix Quotes," BrainyQuote, accessed August 18, 2021, https://www.brainyquote.com/authors/jimi-hendrix-quotes.

Chapter 10

1. Maarten de Kadt, *The Bronx River: An Environmental and Social History* (Charleston, SC: History Press, 2011).

2. *Bronx River Restoration: Master Plan* (The Bronx, January 1, 1980).

3. T. Suvendrini Lena, et al., "Elemental Carbon and PM(2.5) Levels in an Urban Community Heavily Impacted by Truck Traffic," *Environmental Health Perspectives* 110, no. 10 (October 2002): 1009–1015.

Chapter 12

1. David R. Williams, Jourdyn A. Lawrence, and Brigette A. Davis, "Racism and Health: Evidence and Needed Research," *Annual Review of Public Health* 40 (April 2019): 105–125.

2. Grace A. Noppert, "COVID-19 Is Hitting Black and Poor Communities the Hardest, Underscoring Fault Lines in Access and Care for Those on Margins," *Conversation*, April 9, 2020, https://theconversation.com /covid-19-is-hitting-black-and-poor-communities-the-hardest-underscoring -fault-lines-in-access-and-care-for-those-on-margins-135615; Sumi M. Sexton et al., "Systemic Racism and Health Disparities: A Statement from Editors of Family Medicine Journals," *Annals of Family Medicine* 19, no. 1 (January/February 2021): 1–3, https://www.annfammed.org/content /annalsfm/19/1/2.full.pdf; and Joe Feagin and Zinobia Bennefield, "Systemic Racism and U.S. Health Care," *Social Science and Medicine* 103 (February 2014): 7–14, https://www.sciencedirect.com/science/article/abs/pii /S0277953613005121.

Chapter 13

1. Issie Lapowsky, "Urban Onshoring: The Movement to Bring Tech Jobs Back to America," *Wired*, November 4, 2014.

Chapter 14

1. "About MacArthur Fellows Program," MacArthur Foundation, accessed August 19, 2021, https://www.macfound.org/programs/fellows /strategy.

Chapter 15

1. Dave Chappelle, 8:46, YouTube, posted by Netflix Is a Joke, June 11, 2020, https://www.youtube.com/watch?v=3tR6mKcBbT4.

Chapter 16

1. *Good Times*, season 2, episode 12, "The Windfall," directed by Herbert Ken, aired December 3, 1974, on CBS.
2. Alexis Stephens, "How Majora Carter Plans to Transform a Building of Injustice in New York," *Next City*, September 29, 2014, https://nextcity .org/daily/entry/majora-carter-spofford-design-new-york-hunts-point.

Chapter 17

1. Alex Frangos, "Affordable-Housing Empire Fuels Developer's Upscale Aims," *Wall Street Journal*, August 22, 2006; and David Gelles, "The Billionaire behind Hudson Yards Thinks New York Is Too Expensive," *New York Times*, August 27, 2020.

Chapter 18

1. Rakhi Bose, "'Gentrify Your Hood': Why Jay-Z's Freestyle Tribute to Nipsey Hussle Is Dividing Fans," *News18.com*, April 19, 2019, https://www.news18.com/news/buzz/why-jay-zs-freestyle-tribute-to -nipsey-hussle-is-dividing-internet-2119961.html.

2. "Slain Teen Remembered at Memorial Addressing Gun Violence," *CBC News*, September 28, 2013, https://www.cbc.ca/news/canada /toronto/slain-teen-remembered-at-memorial-addressing-gun-violence -1.1872107/.

3. Nurith Aizenman, "Gun Violence Deaths: How The U.S. Compares with the Rest of the World," NPR, March 24, 2021, https://www .npr.org/sections/goatsandsoda/2021/03/24/980838151/gun-violence -deaths-how-the-u-s-compares-to-the-rest-of-the-world; and "America's Gun Culture in Charts," BBC, April 8, 2021, https://www.bbc.com/news /world-us-canada-41488081.

4. "Finch West Light Rail Transit," Infrastructure Ontario, accessed May 23, 2021, https://www.infrastructureontario.ca/Finch-West-Light -Rail-Transit.

5. To learn more, the full agreement is available on the Toronto Community Benefits Network website, https://www.communitybenefits .ca/finchwestlrt.

6. "Finch West," Infrastructure Ontario.

7. "About Us," The Colored Girls Museum, accessed August 19, 2021, http://thecoloredgirlsmuseum.com/about-2/.

Chapter 19

1. Elizabeth Streb, "Born to Fly: Elizabeth Streb vs. Gravity," STREB, video, 1:45, accessed July 20, 2021, https://streb.org/elizabeth-streb/.

2. David S. Jackson, "Dune Lankard: Scream of the Little Bird," *Time*, January 11, 1999, http://content.time.com/time/world/article/0,8599 ,2040002,00.html.

Epilogue

1. Mark 12:30–31.

ACKNOWLEDGMENTS

I am a blessed woman.

I give all honor and praise to God for the opportunity to live and love out loud. I've been showered with favor as evidenced by all the people who have contributed to my life in one way, shape, or form and to my ability to write this book.

Marta Rodriguez, a colleague at Sustainable South Bronx, the first person I ever heard say "We shouldn't have to move out of our neighborhood to live in a better one": Thank you for so beautifully and simply encapsulating everything I felt about my life's work and for the inspiration for this book's subtitle.

Mommy and Daddy, Tinnie and Major Wade Carter: I thank you for loving me into existence and caring for me, especially when things were tough for all of us. I feel your presence every day.

My niece Njeri and her mom, my sister Jackie: Thank you for always being mom, sister, or friend to me exactly as I needed.

Pastor Rich and Frances Rivera, Lady Mico/Migdalia Cruz, Suncadm Bey, Tim Soerens, Christiana Rice, and Heather Bickel Stevenson: You are my spiritual warriors and guides.

Seth Godin, Roberta Gratz, Carlton Brown, Linda Conin Gross, Hugh Hogan, Frank and Audrey Peterman, Barry Segal, Kathy Wilde, Earl Washington, Robert Caro, Katya and Maarten DeKadt, Dean and Anne Ornish, Amy Koppleman, Jeanine Basinger, Senator Kirsten Gillibrand, Evert Verhagen, Kyle Alexander OBE, Ariella

Masboungi, Jorge Cancela, Henry McKoy, Kathryn Finney, Evie Lovett, and Jeff Shumlin: You have inspired and supported me in ways that are too numerous to count.

Kimberly Lewis, Dianne Dillon-Ridgley, Michelle Moore, Dr. Mildred (Mama Bahati) McClain, and Melissa Lomba: You all taught me what love leadership looks like.

My Boogie Down Grind Familia: You were my home away from home and you all proved what I knew all along: brilliance shines in our hood.

The Majora Carter Fan Club: Thanks for always thinking of me!

Lenny, Uncle Levi, Yolanda Garcia, Leslie Lowe, Megan Charlop, Judy Bonds, Pam Dashiell, Mrs. Natalie Transport, Mrs. Martha Boyd, Sister Thomas, Pat D'Angelis, and Jonathan Demme: You are my ancestors now and your lessons fuel me daily.

Freda Rosen and group: You taught me that being a powerful Black woman could be a dynamic group effort.

Janine Simon Daughtry, aka J-9: Thank you for being such a great friend all these years—I'm so glad we were enrolled in the same freshman Spanish class at Bronx Science back in 1984!

James Burling Chase: I don't need a hero, but you make me feel like I have one. I love you.

The founder and senior editor of Berrett-Koehler Publishers, Steve Piersanti, once told me I would have a problem because he knew I had way more than one book in me and it would be hard to figure out which book to write first. He was right! Thank you, Steve, for your patience and kindness and for believing in me. You are the best editorial coach ever! I am deeply grateful to you and the team at BK that poured their care and talent into my book.

And to the countless number of people I have met over the years who encouraged me with a good word, a blessing, a painting, a secret, a letter, a poem, cookies, a song, or lots of other beautiful things, I thank you for sharing your talents and your heart with me. I will treasure you always.

And to all my sisters and brothers in low-status communities everywhere, you are ones you've been waiting for.

INDEX

Page references followed by *f* indicate an illustrated figure; those followed by *t* indicate a table.

ABOUT THE AUTHOR

Majora Carter is the youngest child of her late mother, Tinnie Johnson Carter, and her father, Major Wade Carter, who was sixty years strong when his tenth child was born in 1966. Coincidentally, her father was the youngest child of his father too—who was also sixty at the time of little Major's birth in 1907! Majora is the literal granddaughter of a slave born in 1856, a historical stone's throw into a past still with us today.

She grew up in the 1970s and '80s, during a period of tragic decline in government services: the closure of fire departments and other essential pillars of functioning society across American cities—but collectively epitomized by her South Bronx surroundings. Her younger years were also a period of great creativity and social ingenuity for the South Bronx. The Black Panthers, block parties, hip-hop, break dancing, and graffiti bookended her youth while she worked diligently to extricate herself from the situation through education.

And yet as the young Majora weathered local conditions resembling Berlin in 1945, in her acceptance speeches for middle school academic awards—preserved on lined paper with notes from teachers—she delivered constant, irrefutable notes of hope and belief in the potential of everyone around her to do more and be better together. This was not a sensible position to take during that time.

At every turn of Majora's life, she has set the goalpost further and further ahead of what those around her see in front of them. Her recollection of a conversation with one of her more prominent admirers, President Bill Clinton—when he reminded her that "There will never be a time when there is no distance between where we are and where we ought to be"—illuminates the internal tension that has propelled her stellar level of accomplishment, which includes a MacArthur "genius" Fellowship, a Peabody Award in broadcasting, top honors in urban design, a tech social enterprise, seven honorary PhDs, and a brilliant array of Google and Yelp reviews plus an Alfresco New York City Award for her hip-hop cafe, the Boogie Down Grind.

Majora is the first to declare that she isn't possessed of any special talents but more likely an emotional inability to ignore inequality, wasted potential, or even a slim chance of success against the odds.

She is quoted on the walls of the Smithsonian's National Museum of African American History and Culture in Washington, DC: *"Nobody should have to move out of their neighborhood to live in a better one"*—a credo she continues to embody, without sanctimony or obligation, because it feeds her insatiable appetite for new challenges, victories, and opportunities to learn and share. It's ironic that her early drive to get out of the South Bronx through education is what eventually equipped and motivated her to return, stay, and build a quality of life that nobody predicted.

Majora's career is not characterized by a string of "problems solved." She has created physical and emotional landscapes where others can more effectively solve the next challenges, create the next solutions nobody expects, learn from failures, and enjoy all of the big moments and small victories along the way.

❀ Berrett–Koehler
BK Publishers

Berrett-Koehler is an independent publisher dedicated to an ambitious mission: *Connecting people and ideas to create a world that works for all.*

Our publications span many formats, including print, digital, audio, and video. We also offer online resources, training, and gatherings. And we will continue expanding our products and services to advance our mission.

We believe that the solutions to the world's problems will come from all of us, working at all levels: in our society, in our organizations, and in our own lives. Our publications and resources offer pathways to creating a more just, equitable, and sustainable society. They help people make their organizations more humane, democratic, diverse, and effective (and we don't think there's any contradiction there). And they guide people in creating positive change in their own lives and aligning their personal practices with their aspirations for a better world.

And we strive to practice what we preach through what we call "The BK Way." At the core of this approach is *stewardship,* a deep sense of responsibility to administer the company for the benefit of all of our stakeholder groups, including authors, customers, employees, investors, service providers, sales partners, and the communities and environment around us. Everything we do is built around stewardship and our other core values of *quality, partnership, inclusion, and sustainability.*

This is why Berrett-Koehler is the first book publishing company to be both a B Corporation (a rigorous certification) and a benefit corporation (a for-profit legal status), which together require us to adhere to the highest standards for corporate, social, and environmental performance. And it is why we have instituted many pioneering practices (which you can learn about at www.bkconnection.com), including the Berrett-Koehler Constitution, the Bill of Rights and Responsibilities for BK Authors, and our unique Author Days.

We are grateful to our readers, authors, and other friends who are supporting our mission. We ask you to share with us examples of how BK publications and resources are making a difference in your lives, organizations, and communities at www.bkconnection.com/impact.

Dear reader,

Thank you for picking up this book and welcome to the worldwide BK community! You're joining a special group of people who have come together to create positive change in their lives, organizations, and communities.

What's BK all about?

Our mission is to connect people and ideas to create a world that works for all.

Why? Our communities, organizations, and lives get bogged down by old paradigms of self-interest, exclusion, hierarchy, and privilege. But we believe that can change. That's why we seek the leading experts on these challenges—and share their actionable ideas with you.

A welcome gift

To help you get started, we'd like to offer you a **free copy** of one of our bestselling ebooks:

www.bkconnection.com/welcome

When you claim your **free ebook**, you'll also be subscribed to our blog.

Our freshest insights

Access the best new tools and ideas for leaders at all levels on our blog at ideas.bkconnection.com.

Sincerely,

Your friends at Berrett-Koehler